High School Latinx
Counternarratives

Critical
Studies of
LATINXS
in the
Americas

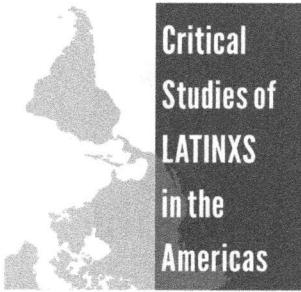

Yolanda Medina and Margarita Machado-Casas
General Editors

Vol. 27

The Critical Studies of Latinxs in the Americas series
is part of the Peter Lang Trade Academic and Textbook list.
Every volume is peer reviewed and meets
the highest quality standards for content and production.

PETER LANG
New York • Bern • Berlin
Brussels • Vienna • Oxford • Warsaw

Juan A. Ríos Vega

High School Latinx Counternarratives

Experiences in School and Post-graduation

PETER LANG

New York • Bern • Berlin
Brussels • Vienna • Oxford • Warsaw

Library of Congress Control Number: 2020945362

Bibliographic information published by **Die Deutsche Nationalbibliothek.**
Die Deutsche Nationalbibliothek lists this publication in the "Deutsche
Nationalbibliografie"; detailed bibliographic data are available
on the Internet at http://dnb.d-nb.de/.

ISSN 2372-6822 (print)
ISSN 2372-6830 (online)
ISBN 978-1-4331-8129-0 (hardcover)
ISBN 978-1-4331-8130-6 (paperback)
ISBN 978-1-4331-8131-3 (ebook pdf)
ISBN 978-1-4331-8132-0 (epub)
ISBN 978-1-4331-8133-7 (mobi)
DOI 10.3726/b17169

In memory of Sheila Sixtos and William Hernandez

My Name

Sheila is my name and it has a weird meaning. It is something about flowers and heaven. I have never paid attention to it; it's just my name, the way people call me. The reason why my parents decided to name me Sheila has a funny story. My mom and my Aunt Patty were pregnant at the same time. One day while they were at the mall buying clothes for the babies, they decided to watch a movie. It was a beautiful movie about a princess from England named Sheila. The story was awesome. It talked about the power of love and dreams. It showed that with love everything is possible. My Aunt loved that name and she decided to name her baby daughter like that. My mom liked the name too, but the doctors had told her that I was going to be a boy. But the funny thing about my name is that I was born first and when the doctors told my mom that I was a girl, she decided to name me Sheila. My Aunt got so mad at my mom because of what she had done. My Aunt didn't talk to my mom for two months until my cousin was born. When her daughter was born, she didn't think about how she was going to name her baby girl. Finally, she named her Mitzi. I know it is a weird name, but it's not that ugly, well compared to mine, it is ugly. But what can I do? I have a smart mom and she got the best name for me. I love my name, but just when people pronounce it correctly, because when they say it wrong, it sounds ugly. I hate when people call me Cheila; my name is

Sheila, like Shhhheila. It is not hard, but they can't say it right. Another thing is that I don't like about my name is how they call me in English. Since I came to live here in the U.S., my name is not Sheila anymore, but Shila. What? I hate it. I tell teachers, "My name is Sheila, Shhheila", but they don't get it. I think I have to get used to it since I live here everything in my life has changed, including my name. Anyway, I love the way my family and friends call me, by my name, Sheila.

(Sheila's journal, January 2008)

Dear Mr. Ríos

My name is William Hernandez. I am 15 years old. I live in the town of Asheboro in North Carolina. I have black hair and brown skin. I am an honest person who likes to respect elders and help others. I like to write and to play soccer.

During the week, I go to school in the mornings. When I return home, I help my mom with the house work first and then I eat. I live with my mom and my sister. We help each other. When I finish helping my mom, sometimes I do homework and listen to music. Since my dad doesn't live with us, we live in a small apartment.

Now, my mother has a boyfriend, who wants to marry her and takes us to Charlotte, so we could have a better life. My sister is 6 years old. She goes to kindergarten. I love her so much because she is cool. Well, sometimes she is mean because she took my place and now every person says that she is cute and everything, so I am not the cute one anymore. Anyways, I am proud to have such a family. This is all I can say about me and my lovely family.

(William's journal, January 2008)

Contents

Figures

CHAPTER ONE

Latinx Voices Counternarratives

As a high school teacher, I had no idea how to save my students from their own lives except to include them in my writing, not for their sake, but for my own. I couldn't undo myself from their stories any other way. How do you get any sleep at night if you witness stories that don't let you go? (Cisneros, 2015, p. 39)

Introduction

It was in the summer of 2017 when I went back to the semi-rural county in North Carolina where I had worked as an English as a second language (ESL) teacher for over 15 years in two different high schools. It was a strange feeling while driving down the streets and recalling familiar places with nostalgia and mixed feelings. I felt like a ghost coming back to visit and to reconnect with my former students. My students and I agreed to meet at the local library, my favorite place since I came to live in the county. I have to admit that reconnecting with my students after 5–10 years was very exciting but at the same time painful. It was also exciting since I wanted to find out what had happened with their lives after they finished high school but painful to hear about their struggles and challenges. I still recall how I went home one night and could not sleep at all after seeing one of students crying for not accomplishing her dreams of becoming a professional in this country. Instead, she ended up working in construction.

Between 1999 and 2012, I taught in a semi-rural county in North Carolina. As a native of Panama, I was able to communicate in both Spanish and English. Although I was aware of my privileged position as a legal immigrant and male teacher, I experienced the same layers of discrimination and racial profiling that most of my students and parents faced in the community. Talking about our personal experiences allow us to develop reciprocal *confianza (trust)*. I also learned to respect my students and their families since they gave me a sense of belonging. In other words, we became a big *familia*.

After ten years, I feel the urgency to document twelve of my former students' narratives and to discuss what happened to them after high school graduation. Since moving into higher education, I have kept most of their writing journals as a personal treasure. During this time, I have been in touch with most of them; some have pursued higher education, some have joined their parents and relatives, working two or three jobs, and others have become new parents. As a new faculty member, I feel the need to analyze these twelve students' journals. I understand the importance of sharing what my students wrote in order to echo how their school experiences prepared or did not prepare them to face life's challenges and/ or higher education. Due to the fact that students of color represent the highest dropout rate in the nation, I see my study with urgency and relevance. I feel this book can be an excellent asset for teachers, school administrators, parents, community leaders, and for anyone who is interested in the educational experience of communities of color in the United States.

The most exciting part of this reencounter with my former students was to show them how I had kept the dialogue journals they wrote when they were in my ESL classroom. Some of them were surprised to realize that I had kept their writing projects for so long. Others even cried while reading their narratives and some others laughed and said things like, "I was so wrong when I wrote it." However, the most important thing about my data collection was the promise I made to my students to document and to publish their histories in this book. Throughout all of these years my students and I have developed a strong friendship through *confianza* (trust) and *respeto* (respect). In this book, I will be using the term "Latinx" as a non-conforming male-female binary.

Theoretical Frameworks

Drawing on critical race theory (CRT), Latino critical theory (LatCrit), and queers of color (QOC) critique, this book analyses how twelve Latinx counterstorytelling narratives intersect multiple layers of oppression in school and society. CRT focuses on the intersectionality of subordination, including gender, class, and other forms of oppression. Challenging Eurocentric epistemology and questioning dominant notions of meritocracy, objectivity, and knowledge have particular application to the field of education, and offer a liberatory pedagogy that encourages inquiry, dialogue, and participation from a wide variety of stakeholders. "Counterstorytelling and narrative serve as a pedagogical tool that allows educators to better understand the experiences of their students of color through deliberate and mindful listening techniques. Learning to listen to these stories and figuring out how to make them matter in the educational system is potentially invigorating and validating" (Taylor, 2009, p. 10). As a highlight, this book also explorest the use of dialogue journaling (Peyton & Reed, 1990) as a classroom writing strategy. When revisited after ten years, to critically analyze the educational experiences of the participants in the study; thus, allowing them to become creators of their own narratives with issues of oppression and resistance during and after they completed high school.

Additionally, as an umbrella under CRT, LatCrit scholars agree that racism, sexism, and classism intersect other layers of oppression based on "immigration status, sexuality, culture, language, phenotype, accent, and surname" (Hernandez-Truyol, Harris, & Valdés, 2015; Stefancic, 1998). Similarly, Solórzano and Yosso (2009) agree that "utilizing the experiences of Latinas/os, a LatCrit theory in education also theorizes and examines that place where racism intersects with other forms of subordination such as sexism, classism, nativism, monolingualism, and heterosexism" (p. 144).

According to Solórzano and Yosso (2009), critical race methodology theoretically, "(a) foregrounds race and racism in all aspects of the research process. It also challenges the separate discourses of race, gender and class by showing how these three elements intersect to affect the experiences of students of color; (b) challenges the traditional research paradigms, texts, theories used to explain the experiences of students of color; (c) offers a liberatory or transformative solution to racial, gender, and class subordination; and (d) focuses on the racialized, gendered, and classed experiences of students of color" (p. 131). QOC critique represents a large pool of interdisciplinary scholarship that explores how resistance has shaped the lives of queer of people of color. QOC critique draws on indigenous studies, Black feminism, as well as Latinx and queer scholars. Claims that QOC critique "seeks to unveil the social and historical forces that have produced QOC marginality, as doing so provides a backdrop for exploring strategies of resistance" (p. 30) based on lived experiences of QOC. In this book, two of the participants, who self-identified as a gay and lesbian Latinx, narrate their personal stories. They share how their sexual orientation intersect homophobia from their parents and relatives and racial discrimination from mainstream society, leading them to face multiple forms of subordination (Cisneros, 2017; Cisneros & Bracho, 2019; Duran & Pérez II, 2017; Ríos Vega & Franeta, 2017).

Dialogue Journals as a Writing Strategy in ESL

Dialogue journaling has been defined as "a written conversation between a teacher and an individual student," focusing on meaning rather than form while developing linguistic and academic competence in a new language (Peyton & Reed, 1990, p. 3). The use of dialogue journals in the ESL classroom has become very popular since it was first introduced, studied, and used by scholars, as well as teachers (Kim, 2011; Mayher, 1990; Nassaji & Cumming, 2000; Peregoy & Boyle, 2017; Staton, Shuy, Peyton, & Reed, 1988). Kim (2011) defines dialogue journal as "the authentic communication between two people" while providing linguistic support in first and second language (p. 27). In English language learners' writing skills, scholars have drawn from Vygotsky's (1978) zone of proximal development (ZPD) that analyzes "the distance between the actual developmental level as determined by independent problem solving and the level of potential development as determined through problem solving under adult guidance or in collaboration with more capable peers" (86). ESL teachers have found the use of dialogue journals as a positive writing strategy to better monitor fluency. In dialogue journaling, teachers do not correct students' errors, instead they prompt students with clarifying questions and providing model of diction, language use, and mechanics about their narratives. Peregoy and Boyle (2017) consider the use of dialogue journal as an "excellent introduction to literacy for English language learners of all ages" (p. 233). Besides improving students' writing skills while choosing and developing their own topics, teachers and students develop a personal relationship. Darhower (2004) suggests that teachers can use dialogue journals as a platform to discuss class-related issues "beyond the walls of the classroom … Teachers can also connect journal content to class discussion by having students share what they write" (p. 334). Peyton and Reed (1990) posit that using dialogue journals allows students "the opportunity to express themselves openly and in private, without being embarrassed about the nature of their concerns or the limits of their language to express themselves" (p. 14). Personally, in my ESL classroom, the use of dialogue journaling became an excellent outlet for my students to make connections with the experiences of Latinx writers and their personal experiences as Latinx immigrants to this country.

Methodology

In this book, I used face-to-face, Skype, and Facebook interviews (Glesne, 2006) to document the experiences of former ESL Latinx students during and post-high school. In addition, I used the participants' dialogue journals (artifacts) (Creswell, 2016) as another form of data to connect them with their high school and lived experiences. First, using their dialogue journals allowed the participants to be able to critically reflect on their educational journey in this country. Then, through the interviews, they were able to discuss whether or not their education in this country prepared them or not to pursue higher education or to climb the social ladder.

Participants

I saved my students' dialogue journals since 2002 and have been in touch with many of them since then. In the summer of 2017, I contacted twelve of them via social media and phone calls. I traveled to North Carolina to conduct most of my face-to-face interviews. After the first face-to-face interviews, I also held Facebook interviews to clarify my data analysis and interpretation. One of the participants in this book (Julio) is currently living in Mexico, so his interviews were held mainly via Skype.

The face-to-face interviews were held at the conference room at a public library in North Carolina. Before the interviews, I organized all of my participants' dialogue journals. At the beginning, each participant was surprised to see that I had kept their journals for such a long time. It set the tone for each of them to reflect their high school experiences and lives in this country. First, I asked them to silently read their journals, pushing them to reconnect with the past. After that, I asked them to share with me what crossed their minds as they were reading their artifacts (Saldaña & Omasta, 2018). Then I continued asking my study leading questions. These open-ended questions also allowed the participants to narrate personal anecdotes about their lives during and post-high school. Each interview lasted approximately ninety minutes.

Data Collection: Dialogue Journals and Leading Questions

Using the participants' dialogue journals and the interviews allowed me to find common patterns in the students' narratives (Creswell & Poth, 2018; Glesne, 2006; Saldaña & Omasta, 2018). First, the participants' journals encouraged them to connect with their (im)migration journeys and experiences as students in this country. Second, the open-ended questions served as a springboard to critically analyze how their educational experiences shaped their lives during and after high school graduation.

Research Questions

Using CRT, LatCrit in education and QOC epistemologies, high school Latinx counternarratives in school and post-graduation, the remainder of this book attempts to focus on the following questions:

1. How does the use of dialogue journaling allow Latinx ESL students to narrate their experiences in high school?
2. How does the intersectionality of race/ethnicity, immigration status, English language, sexual orientation, and other social issues shape Latinx' experiences in high school?
3. How does the educational experience of Latinx students in high school prepare them to pursue post-secondary education and access upper social mobility?

These research questions allowed me to develop open-ended questions and analyze the participants' journals. I organized the participants' journals and narratives into three main themes and sub-themes that they raised during our interviews and dialogue journals analysis. I personally decided to transcribe all of the data since most of the participants chose to speak in Spanish, only two of them carried the whole interview in English. After the interviews were transcribed and coded, I also coded the participants' dialogue journals. As a result, I developed three main themes and sub-themes—(im)migration journey: border crossers, leaving the island(s), parents and relatives; navigating high school: discrimination and racism, tracking and low expectations, teachers and classes; and resiliency after high school: college and Deferred Action for Childhood Arrivals (DACA), undocuqueers, new families and jobs, and paying back.

Unpacking My Positionality

As a post-critical ethnographer, I was also conscious about my positionality, reflexivity, and objectivity. "Cultures are not objects in any simple sense. They are ephemeral and multiple while our interpretations are always partial and positional" (Noblit, Flores, & Murillo, 2004, p. 22). I was critically aware of my race/ethnicity, class, privilege as a former ESL teacher, immigration status, and bilingualism in relation to my participants. I was also conscious about that my participants and I share similar cultural backgrounds and lived experiences as Latinx immigrants to this country. These experiences allowed me to become an "insider" and to relate closely to most of my participants and their families. Additionally, I was aware of my "outsider" role to mainstream society since I have also experienced most of the same racial profiling discrimination that most of my participants in this book have been through. It was my subjectivity as an "insider" and "outsider" to both the participants and the mainstream society that pushed me to analyze my own feelings in relationship to what I learned about myself and what kept me from learning. Since the participants used to be my students and the artifacts used in this study were developed in my ESL classroom, I realized that I had to pay constant attention to my subjectivity. My subjectivity allowed me to learn from my participants' narratives as they shared parts of their lives with me, especially about things that happened in their lives while they were still my students and I was not aware of. I was also cognizant about of my emotions when my participants unpacked issues of injustice and inequality while attending college and becoming aware of their immigration obstacles to pursue higher education. Additionally, it was my subjectivity that led to critically analyze my own journey as a male immigrant to this country, my family values, education, and professional life. Finally, my subjectivity pushed me to see myself as a researcher while analyzing the participants' counternarratives and the selection of themes through the writing of this book.

As a post-critical ethnographer, my reflexivity allowed me to analyze how my former students' lives and ways of thinking had changed since I taught them. Through our conversations we were able to engage in critical thoughts about their education and its impact after they graduated from high school. My reflexivity also encouraged me to ask questions about my role as the participants' former teacher and about myself as I wrote in my reflections. I was constantly questioning my own journey and privilege as an immigrant first and then naturalized citizen to this country. During the interviewing process, my reflexivity also led me to reveal my sexual orientation as a queer of color to two of my participants, allowing them to share personal and sensitive issues about gender and sexual identities in the Latinx communities. Throughout my reflexivity, I was always concerned about my study and the type of data that I was getting from the participants (Glesne, 2006).

Using Creswell and Poth's (2018) narrative research strategies, I developed some questions that allowed my students to reflect on their educational experience and that would help me analyze what happened to them during and after they finished high school. Since I already knew them, it was easy for me to determine which stories needed to be documented as part of this book. Previous to the interviews, I was able to read and to analyze their dialogue journals, allowing me to prepare more specific questions about their educational experience in the U.S.

In order to reconnect my former students with their high school education and their ESL class, I showed them their dialogue journals as a springboard for them to recall and to critically reflect on their former education. Through face-to-face interviews the participants were able to talk about their past, present, and their future (Clandinin & Connelly, 2000). Each interviewed lasted between 1 or 2 hours. Interviewing my former students allowed me to ask questions about themselves, their parents, and sometimes new families. Since most of the participants decided to answer the interview questions in Spanish, I felt it was important for me to transcribe and to start analyzing them as well. Once I finished transcribing the interviews, I started developing "individual stories within the participants' personal experiences" (Creswell & Poth, 2018, p. 72). Then the participants' experiences were reorganized in a chronological order (beginning, middle, and end), allowing me to come out with themes and sub-themes. In order to collaborate with the stories, the participants and I analyzed and negotiated the different preliminary themes that I developed, adding validation check to the analysis.

Literature Review about Latinx Education

Latinx youth account for a growing percentage of the United States' student population as immigration policies continue to shape the geopolitical and sociocultural landscape in education (Noguera, Hurtado, & Fergus, 2013). When Latinx youth enroll in schools, they are oftentimes met with hostile curricula, school staff, and communities that are unsupportive and deter students from succeeding inside and beyond the classroom. For instance, for Latino males, the role of education remains somewhat distanced as these young men must face tougher and immediate hardships that de-prioritize education for the sake of their families and personal lives (Lopez, 2003).

Unlike other large student groups in America, Latinx youth are also additionally confronted with the issue of their legality as those students who are undocumented immigrants fear family separation due to deportation (Golash-Boza, 2015; Gonzales, 2016). While the scholarly literature on the challenges Latinx confront in educational contexts is rich, less research is discussed about how these students persevere and navigate through these challenges in healthy and productive ways. This literature review will examine the various challenges Latinx encounter in school with teacher expectations and absenteeism, their family and personal struggles, and the issue of legality and its toll on mental/emotional health.

Teacher Expectations

The general public tends to revere schools as welcoming and warm learning spaces where students develop and strengthen their cognitive and social skills. Schools are held in high regard as academic institutes comprised of rigorous curricula and supportive staff that encourage students' educational potential. However, research suggests that schools may not necessarily be as receptive to the cultural, linguistic, and social demographics of Latinx students. In fact, teachers' expectations of Latinx influence how these students navigate their schooling experiences and attitudes toward faculty and learning (Avilés, Guerrero, Howarth, & Thomas, 1999; Brewster & Bowen, 2004; Conchas, 2001; Constantine, Kindaichi, & Miville, 2007; Fernandez, 2002; López, 2003; Sánchez, Colón, & Esparza, 2005).

Some teachers underestimate the potential and abilities of these students which unfortunately could lead to students fulfilling the low expectations teachers hold against them. Furthermore, these low expectations may even push students away from valuing an education. When students are consciously aware that their teachers have widespread low expectations of their academic achievement, students are more likely to not view education as valuable (Sánchez et al., 2005). Conchas (2001) mentions further how teachers' low expectations and "lack of cultural awareness" work in sync to detriment the academic progress of Latinx (p. 476). Teachers largely unaware of students' intersectional identities teaching a curriculum that is culturally incongruent to students' cultural and personal lives leaves many students feeling disconnected and unattached to learning.

Brewster and Browen (2004) even posit that "teacher support may also be of greater importance to Latinx than to those from other racial or ethnic backgrounds, because White teachers may have less understanding of Latino culture" (p. 51). With a teaching workforce that is predominantly female and White, Latino males are disproportionately disadvantaged. Some scholars even suggest that academic interventions for students of color and teachers be conducted to enhance cognitive skills and reduce the widening achievement gap (Caldwell & Siwatu, 2003).

Conversely, these low expectations have also been found to strengthen the resolve of Latinx students to persevere despite the low confidence from their teachers (Ríos Vega, 2015). In the classroom, Latino males may even feel pressured to counter these low expectations by outperforming other students (Constantine et al., 2007). Teacher expectations lead to students having to prove their academic worth on a larger scale as Latinx students are not only succeeding in the classroom for themselves, but for the sake of their families and larger cultural and racial group. Yet, this behavior adds more stress into the lives of Latinx students already confronting racism and discrimination in society. For some, this stress begins to affect their daily attendance in school.

Absenteeism & Dropping Out

According to Torres and Fergus (2012), the school structure, lowered academic expectations, language barriers, home-school incompatibility, and the cultural incongruity of the curricula all factor into Latinx absenteeism. In *Subtractive Schooling: U.S.-Mexican Youth and the Politics of Caring*, Valenzuela (1999) examines how school politics and teacher care influence students' intrinsic motivation, willingness, and propensity to succeed within the classroom. Valenzuela (1999) found that curricula which ignore students' cultural and linguistic identities—as well as their community-based knowledge—perform educational malpractice. In other words, Latinx students are more likely to view school and learning as "uninteresting [and] irrelevant" if they do not feel a personal connection to the learning material (p. 62). The impersonal nature of the structural barriers in school leads many Latinx youth to not attend classes regularly (Avilés et al., 1999). Irregular school attendance does harm to a students' ability to not only graduate, but also learn. Unfortunately, Latinx then drop out of school.

The difficulty of completing schoolwork and the lack of English proficiency levels among immigrant youth and some Latinx also cause students to fall behind their peers and eventually drop out. While Latinx youth may be more familiar with the social language of English, they may struggle with competency in the academic language used in textbooks and spoken/written in classes (Behnke, Gonzalez, & Cox, 2010). According to Gándara and Contreras (2010), Latinx students are more likely to reside in households where their parents are not native English speakers. Consequently, these families may have a harder time communicating with school teachers and staff members about their child's progress in school. This communication gap ultimately can increase the likelihood of Latinx students dropping out of school (Gándara & Contreras, 2010). Other risk factors for dropping out include family mobility, job and home responsibilities, peer pressure, and personal risk factors such as pregnancy or home stressors (Avilés et al., 1999; Behnke et al., 2010; López, 2003; Saunders & Serna, 2004; Ríos Vega, 2015).

Family mobility is another common cause for students dropping out of school. Some students' parents may not find a stable place of residence, which causes students to migrate from place to place, leaving schools and friends behind in search of a new place to call home. Other students may have work responsibilities that interfere with their ability to complete coursework and attend classes. For instance, when large numbers of Latino males drop out of high school, they lose the trajectory of attending colleges and universities in the United States (Torres & Fergus, 2012). But for first-generation Latinx students, they may lack the knowledge of university culture to fully take advantage of the resources, tools, and interpersonal relationships between students and professors to succeed in colleges and universities (Saunders & Serna, 2004). Schools are not the only places where Latinx students are presented with challenges.

Family & Personal Struggles

Latinx not only face a myriad of challenges in their schools, but they are also exposed to struggles in their households, communities, and personal lives. Saenz and Ponjuán (2009) share how there is a salient expectation for Latinx to join the workforce in order to provide for and support their families. These additional duties often interfere and disrupt the schooling process as Latinx youth—especially immigrants—may have to re-prioritize life responsibilities in order to survive and take care of loved ones. Many immigrant families may also live in low-income communities with poorer resources and social support systems (Gándara & Contreras, 2009). For instance, some families may be thrust into a cycle of generational poverty, and some Latino males may find solace in the streets, joining gangs in order to sell drugs and support their family financially (Conchas, 2001; De Genova & Ramos-Zayas, 2003; Golash-Boza, 2015; López, 2003; Ríos Vega, 2015; Vigil, 2012).

While education still holds intrinsic value among Latino families, it becomes less of an immediate concern as immigrant families struggle for employment, belongingness, and a sense of security in a new country. Many children who arrive to the United States travel with their parents, guardians, and some have even traveled alone. Qualitative research also shows that immigration status influences students' decisions to drop out of school (Avilés et al., 1999; Conchas, 2001; Gándara & Contreras, 2009). Undocumented Latinx may feel uncertainty and fear for their families. Some immigrants arrive to America in hopes of fulfilling the proclaimed American Dream, but threats and concerns of deportation loom near. In addition, lacking legal citizenship prohibits students from college enrollment (Gándara & Contreras, 2009).

Participants Profiles

I chose twelve participants for my book, representing different cultural backgrounds, gender, immigration status, sexual orientation, and social status. It is important to highlight that the participants' names are pseudonyms to protect their vulnerability as communities of color.

Pseudonyms	Country of Origin	Years in the US	Current Age	Immigration Status	Sexual Identity
Mauricio	Puerto Rico/ US territory	5	20	US citizen	Heterosexual
Gloria	Mexico	9	27	Undocumented	Heterosexual
Esperanza	Guatemala	11	24	Undocumented	Heterosexual
Elisa	Dominican Republic	13	29	Naturalized Citizen	Heterosexual
Santiago	Dominican Republic	13	26	Naturalized Citizen	Heterosexual
Francisco	Mexico	13	27	Undocumented	Heterosexual
Diana	Honduras	16	28	Undocumented	Heterosexual
Antonio	Mexico	15	26	Undocumented	Gay
Dulce	Mexico	15	32	Undocumented	Lesbian
Sofia	El Salvador	13	27	Undocumented	Heterosexual
Lúz	Mexico	19	28	Undocumented	Heterosexual
Julio	Mexico	9	28	Undocumented	Heterosexual

Mauricio

Mauricio migrated from Puerto Rico to live with some relatives to avoid gang-related problems on the island. First, Mauricio attended a newcomer school for newly arrived immigrants and ESL students. Then he was sent to a mainstream high school where he experienced invisibility and low expectations from classroom teachers. Mauricio narrated how he felt as a high school student, sometimes ignored and/or labeled Mexican for speaking English with a Spanish accent and skin tone. After finishing high school, Mauricio decided to attend a local community college where he realized how ill-prepared he was to pursue higher education. Finally, he dropped out of college and started working in a mattress factory. Later, he decided to attend a private school to become a professional barber.

Dulce

Dulce came to reunite with her parents after almost three years. Dulce talked about her challenges while attending high school in the US. Back in Mexico she was a senior; however, due to her English level, she was considered a freshman student in the US. At the beginning, Dulce shares how she struggled with her new language, school culture, and lack of empathy from teachers while she was asked to speak English instead of her native language. While being a high school student, Dulce also worked part-time and second shift at a fast-food restaurant. She used to drive her younger siblings to school every day to support her family since she was the oldest of five children. As an undocumented youth who came to the US after turning 16, Dulce could not qualify for DACA. Additionally, Dulce unpacked how sexual orientation and being undocumented shape Latinx young adults after high school. Finally, Dulce shared how she had to negotiate her sexual orientation and female partner with her parents to resist homophobia from her own kinship and racism from mainstream society.

Francisco

Francisco was born in Veracruz, México and came to the US at the age of 16. Like Dulce, he could not benefit from DACA. While attending high school, he also worked at a local fast-food restaurant as a part-time employee. Due to the fact that he did not benefit from DACA and lack of monetary support to pursue higher education, he had no choice but to continue working at the same fast-food restaurant until he and other undocumented young adults were laid off for not having a legal immigration status. By the time of my last interview, Francisco was working with his relatives in construction, hoping to open a family business to support his stay at-home mother and youngest brother.

Elisa

Elisa was born in the Dominican Republic and moved to North Carolina at age 16 along with her parents and her brother Santiago in 2005. Elisa's challenges in high school focused more on breaking stereotypes against Latinx students. As an Afro-Latina, she experienced a lot of invisibility and embarrassment at school, especially when teachers asked her to present her projects in front of the class. The fact that Elisa decided to graduate a semester early from high school and being placed in unchallenging courses due to her English language proficiency made her college journey even more difficult.

After graduating from high school, Elisa enrolled at a local community college and completed her associate degree. Then, she transferred to a local university where she finished her undergraduate in Fashion Design. Elisa's self-identity as a Latina and Dominican, as well as her parents' support, encouraged her to become resilient and to challenge discrimination and low expectations toward Latinx students in education and mainstream society.

Santiago

Santiago is Elisa's brother. When he came to North Carolina, he was 14 years old; however, he looked like a middle school Latino boy. At the beginning, he suffered from cultural shock. Like Elisa, Santiago also suffered discrimination at school due to his lack of English and lack of empathy from teachers.

After he graduated from high school, he started working at a fast-food restaurant. After a year, he attended a local community college to study Graphic Design. While in college, Santiago felt isolated and discriminated for being the only Latino student in the class. He shared how his professors paid more attention to White students than to him. He shared how the fact that he was not advised to take challenging courses while in high school affected his college journey.

After experiencing frustration and invisibility, Santiago decided to drop out of college to work at different temporary jobs.

Diana

Diana was born in Honduras and after being raised by her grandmother back in her homeland, she reunited with her parents after 10 years. The fact that Diana lived most of her childhood with her grandmother made it difficult for her to get used to her parents and the new country. Diana's father was a pastor at a local Christian church, so she had no choice but to follow her parents' religious beliefs and house rules. Her introverted personality also made it difficult for her to make friends and to develop her English language.

After high school graduation, Diana's parents decided to keep her at home, helping her mother around the house for over three years. It was Diana's goal to study Cosmetology; however, the fact that she was undocumented and her lack of information about college from counselors and parental support made it hard to pursue her dreams. Later, Diana decided to leave her house to move in with a Mexican family as a result of her parents' disapproval of her boyfriend. At age 27, Diana lives with her husband and two children. She is a stay at-home mother, taking care of her two children and husband.

Antonio

Antonio is Francisco's brother. Antonio has always been very effeminate. While in high school, he used to like to hang out with Latinas. He shared how he experienced segregation from being Latino more than for his sexual orientation at school. Like most of the students in this book, Antonio shared how being in the ESL classroom gave him a sense of belonging and freedom to be himself. He also shared how he was able to meet and befriend students from different cultural backgrounds while learning English in the ESL classroom. Antonio's journey as an undocumented boy (11 years old) was shocking since his mother, who was already living and working in North Carolina, did not know that he was crossing the border with a "coyote" (smuggler).

Although Antonio experienced invisibility and segregation, he also took care of family obligations while attending high school. Like his brother, Antonio worked part-time at the same fast-food restaurant. After graduation, he continued working at the same fast-food restaurant as a full-time employee until he moved to a larger city in the South to work at a retail store.

Due to the fact that Antonio was granted a social security number and work permit as a DACA recipient made his way easier to access a decent job. Antonio's narrative also shows his experiences as a gay Latino. He shared how he has suffered more discrimination for being Latino than for being gay. He also talked about how he negotiated his homosexuality with his Catholic mother and brothers.

Sofia

Sofia was born in El Salvador. After living with her grandmother for over 10 years, Sofia's parents paid a "coyote" (smuggler) to bring her to the US. After leaving her homeland at age 14, Sofia narrated how she crossed the borders between El Salvador and Guatemala, and then Mexico, until she joined her parents in North Carolina. She also talked about her difficulties while getting used to her parents after being raised by her grandmother, who she used to refer to her grandmother as her real mother. She shared how she wanted to go back to El Salvador. Sofia preferred to spend a lot of time by herself instead of demanding her parents why they left her for such a long time back in her homeland. Her educational experience in the US, like most immigrant students, was frustrating at the beginning due to not being able to speak the English language. She narrated how being in her ESL class and having a Spanish-speaking ESL teacher allowed her to find *familism* and acceptance. She also talked about her panic attacks once she started attending high school as a result of not being able to understand the English language and experiencing culture shock.

After finishing high school, Sofia decided to pursue higher education at the local community college; however, due to her immigration status as undocumented, she had to pay out-of-state tuition. Then she started working full-time at a fast-food restaurant until she became a manager. In 2011, Sofia applied to DACA and received her social security number and work permit. During those years, Sofia had her first child. Unfortunately, her boyfriend (a White man) ended their relationship a few months after she had her son. Sofia is currently studying Business Administration online, working full-time, and raising her son.

Esperanza

Esperanza is a Mesoamerican girl from Guatemala. She shared all of her obstacles while crossing the borders to come to the U.S. Esperanza came to live with some relatives who ended up abusing her physically until she decided to escape and asked for help. Esperanza narrated how she ended up being taken to the Department of Social Services where she met a foster mother, a White, Christian woman. Attending high school was a big challenge for Esperanza due to the fact that she could not communicate in English or Spanish since she spoke "*acateco*," a Mesoamerican indigenous language. Neither being able to speak Spanish or English made her a victim of bullying and discrimination from mainstream students and other Spanish-speaking peers. Due to the fact that she lived with a native English speaker, Esperanza's literacy skills in spoken English were more obvious than her Spanish. As a result, some of her Spanish-speaking friends used to discriminate against her, saying that she pretended to be White. However, Esperanza found refuge in sports, allowing her to overcome mental breakdowns and discrimination.

After finishing high school, Esperanza continued her college education at the local community college since her initial goal was to become an athletic trainer. Moving from high school to college was not easy for Esperanza since she did not have the same support system that her foster mother had created for her while she was in high school. As a result, she spent three years at the community college. She kept dropping out and changing courses that she found very difficult due to their high academic English level. Currently, Esperanza is attending a private university, trying to complete her degree in Criminal Justice with a minor in Law Enforcement. She regrets that some of the courses she took while in high school did not prepare her to face the challenges (language) that she encountered and still does as a university student.

Gloria

Gloria was born in México. Like most of the participants in this book, Gloria experienced bullying and invisibility in school for not being able to speak the English language. Because of that, she ended up taking basic courses that did not prepare her for college. When she realized that she needed AP or advanced courses in order to pursue higher education, she was already a senior student. She shared how she never had a conference with her counselor to talk about college. However, she found in her ESL teacher a role model who encouraged her to pursue higher education.

After obtaining her high school diploma, Gloria decided to go back to Mexico by herself to pursue her academic dreams. After four years, Gloria obtained her undergraduate diploma in Communications and Media in Mexico. Gloria's journey back to Mexico was not easy due to the fact that she was already accustomed to living in the US. Although her English language was not perfect by the time she graduated from high school, she was more literate (writing) in English than in her mother tongue. She referred to it as *"Ni de Aquí, ni de Allá"* (Not from here, Not from there). She studied in a private (Mormon) university under very strict rules and regulations. By the time of our last interview, Gloria was visiting her parents in North Carolina. She was thinking about pursuing a master's degree back in Mexico.

Luz

Luz moved from Mexico when she was nine years old. She shared how she reunited with her father after seven years. When Luz came from Mexico, she attended 4th grade. She shared how she was given silent lunch for not bringing her homework. She explained that because she did not understand English, she could not do her assignments at home. While in high school, she talked about her experiences in math, which she also found challenging. Like others, she also shared how she found her ESL classroom as a nurturing space where she and other students found a sense of belonging and family. In addition, she discovered her love toward reading while being exposed to Latinx writers in the ESL class. Luz used to love dancing Mexican cumbia and organizing local social events. Later, she started attending a Christian church and forgot about dancing and partying. During our last interview, she explained how hard she had to work when she was in high school. She helped her mother to make Mexican food as a family business. She used to stay up until late during the week and to get up early the next day to attend school. She realized that helping her mother in the kitchen took a lot of time away from her studies.

After high school, Luz started working full-time in a local factory. She also runs a part-time business where she sells household artifacts. Luz attended the local community college as a part-time student for over two years, taking online classes. Then she got sick, missing many days of school, which ended up hindering her semester. For that reason, she was not allowed to take her final exams. Being the youngest child out of six and the only unmarried one in her family has put a lot of responsibility on her. By the time of our last interview, she was living and supporting her sick parents. Luz feels that taking care of her parents is her only way to pay them back for all they did for her and her siblings.

Julio

Julio was born in Veracruz, México and while in North Carolina, he become trapped in a system of low expectations, hypermasculinity, and profiling boys of color in elementary school until he finally decided to drop out of high school due to drugs, gang affiliation problems, and lack of school counseling. After breaking the law in the community, he got in trouble with the police after hitting a policeman. He had no choice but to file self-deportation papers or to go to jail at age 17. When Julio decided to go back to his hometown, he realized that his father, who had already been deported, had a new family. Finally, Julio gave himself a second chance and graduated from high school. During our last interview, Julio talked about his job as an auto mechanic in a large farming equipment company and his undergraduate studies. He also shared his good news of becoming a father.

Summary

As I explained in the final remarks of my previous book on Latino teenage boys in education (Ríos Vega, 2015), that although most teachers agreed that more Latino boys are obtaining a high school diploma, few studies have documented what happens to Latinx students after high school graduation. It is important to acknowledge that while some studies have addressed how some Latinx students cannot pursue higher education due to their immigration status and/or financial support, others have documented how first-generation Latinx students' experiences in higher education shape their lives as Latinx (Yosso, Smith, Ceja, & Solórzano, 2009); and other scholars have addressed Latino males experiences in higher education (Sáenz, Ponjuán, & López Figueroa, 2016). However, few studies have voiced the experiences of Latinx after high school. Like the teachers interviewed in my previous study, mainstream statistics indicate that Latinx students are graduating from high school more than other minoritized students; however, few academic studies have followed up what happens to them once they complete their k-12 education in this country. Unfortunately, many of them have to deal with issues of immigration status, lack of financial and familial support while others realize how a subtractive educational system (Valenzuela, 1999) ill-prepared them to pursue higher education and/or to find a decent job.

This book adds to the current literature based on CRT and LatCrit, and QOC critique to explore Latinx students' experiences in education during and post-high school. This book's goal is to echo the silent and invisible voices of Latinx students, especially those who work hard enough to complete their high school education regardless of their immigration status, race/ethnicity, gender, socio-economic status, and sexual orientation. It also analyzes how the participants in this book developed their own resiliency to face personal and social challenges after high school.

Overview of the Chapters

This book closely examines the counternarratives of twelve Latinx and ESL students, their experiences during and after high school graduation. Through the use of dialogue journal as a writing strategy in the ESL classroom, the participants reflect on their (im)migration journeys, educational experiences, and life post-high school graduation. Its goal is to help educators, school administrators, scholars, and other interested audience to better understand how these participants' journeys. While coming to this country looking for a better future, these participants encounter and counteract sociocultural issues, making their goals and dreams difficult to be met. This book is organized into five chapters.

Chapter One *Introduction* focuses on the reason why I decided to develop my study. Drawing from CRT, LatCrit, and QOC epistemologies, I explain the theoretical frameworks and methodology that lead the study. I also explain how the use of dialogue journals and interviews as data collection allowed me to document and to analyze the participants' counternarratives in this book. Additionally, I include the leading questions used to develop my study, as well as my positionality. Then I include a literature review about Latinx education that explores what other scholars have done previously about this topic. Finally, I include the participants' profiles, including a short biography about their cultural and social backgrounds.

Chapter Two *(Im) migration Journey* talks about the participants' counternarratives about their (im)migration experiences while coming to America. Most of the participants came to this country as border crossers from Central America and México, while three others came from the Dominican Republic and Puerto Rico (US territory). This chapter also includes how the relationship with their parents and relatives affect their (im)migration decision.

Chapter Three *Navigating High School* discusses how the participants' educational experience in this country intersects issues of racial profiling, low expectations, language, and tracking. In addition, the participants' share how racism, classism, gender discrimination, and immigration status shape their education and lives after high school. Additionally, two participants unpacked how they used social media to talk about their sexual orientation and how it shaped their relationship with their parents after they finished high school. They also shared about their personal experiences as an undocumented and gay/lesbian, which I will be referring as Undocuqueer, has affected their lives after high school. Other participants shared about their (new) family responsibilities, while others talk about paying their parents back for their sacrifices. This chapter also explores how the participants' similar cultural background with their ESL teacher shape their educational experience while nurturing trust, caring, and love.

Chapter Four *Post-High School* analyzes the participants' counternarratives after high school graduation. It explores how their educational experiences in this country equipped them, or not, to pursue higher education and/or to find decent jobs. The participants revealed how their legal immigration status in this country deterred their aspirations to pursue higher education. Others share how issues of invisibility, racism, and lack of support pushed them to quit attending local community colleges.

Chapter Five *Conclusion, Implications, and Final Words* answers the research questions that led this book. I also analyze my implications that CRT, LatCrit and QOC critique may show for dominant and deficit thinking model school systems and the country's immigration policies toward undocumented, especially Latinx students. I close my book with some final words for school administrators, teachers, parents, and other stakeholders to better prepare Latinx students in order to achieve academic success and climb up the social ladder.

References

Avilés, R. M. D., Guerrero, M. P., Howarth, H. B., & Thomas, G. (1999). Perceptions of Chicano/Latino students who have dropped out of school. *Journal of Counseling & Development, 77*(4), 465–473.

Behnke, A. O., Gonzalez, L. M., & Cox, R. B. (2010). Latino students in new arrival states: Factors and services to prevent youth from dropping out. *Hispanic Journal of Behavioral Sciences, 32*(3), 385–409.

Brewster, A. B., & Bowen, G. L. (2004). Teacher support and the school engagement of Latino middle and high school students at risk of school failure. *Child and Adolescent Social Work Journal, 21*(1), 47–67.

Caldwell, L. D., & Siwatu, K. O. (2003). Promoting academic persistence in African American and Latino high school students: The educational navigation skills seminar in an upward bound program. *The High School Journal, 87*(1), 30–38.

Cisneros, J. (2017). Working with the complexity and refusing to simplify: Undocuqueer meaning making at the intersection of LGBTQ and immigrant rights discourses. *Journal of Homosexuality, 65*(11), 1415–1434. doi: 10.1080/00918369.2017.1380988

Cisneros, S. (2015). *A house of my own: Stories from my life.* New York: Vintage Books, a Division of Penguin Random House LLC.

Cisneros, J., & Bracho, C. (2019). Coming out of the shadows and the closet: Visibility schemas among undocuqueer immigrants. *Journal of homosexuality, 66*(6), 715–734.

Clandinin, D. J., & Connelly, F. M. (2000). *Narrative inquiry: Experience and story of qualitative research.* San Francisco, CA: Jossey-Bass.

Conchas, G. (2001). Structuring failure and success: Understanding the variability in Latino school engagement. *Harvard Educational Review, 71*(3), 475–505.

Constantine, M., Kindaichi, M., & Miville, M. (2007). Factors influencing the educational and vocational transitions of Black and Latino high school students. *Professional School Counseling, 10*(3), 261–265.

Creswell, J. W. (2016). *30 essential skills for the qualitative researcher*: Thousand Oaks, CA: Sage.

Creswell, J. W., & Poth, C. N. (2018). *Qualitative inquiry & research design: Choosing among five approaches* (4th ed.). Thousand Oaks, CA: Sage.

Darhower, M. (2004). Dialogue journals as mediators of l2 learning: A sociocultural account. *Hispania, 87*(2), 324–335.

De Genova, N., & Ramos-Zayas, A. Y. (2003). *Latino crossings: Mexicans, Puerto Ricans, and the politics of race and citizenship*. New York, NY: Routledge.

Duran, A., & Pérez, D. II. (2017). Queering la familia: A phenomenological study reconceptualizing familial capital for queer Latino men. *Journal of College Student Development, 58*(8), 1149–1165.

Fernández, L. (2002). Telling stories about school: Using critical race and Latino critical theories to document Latina/Latino education and resistance. *Qualitative Inquiry, 8*(1), 45–65.

Gándara, P. C., & Contreras, F. (2009). *The Latino education crisis: The consequences of failed social policies*. Cambridge, MA: Harvard University Press.

Gándara, P. C., & Contreras, F. (2010). The Latino education crisis: The consequences of failed social policies. *Educational Leadership, 67*(5), 24–30.

Glesne, C. (2006). *Becoming qualitative researchers: An introduction* (3rd ed.). Upper Saddle River, NJ: Pearson.

Golash-Boza, T. M. (2015). *Deported: Immigrant policing, disposable labor and global capitalism*. New York: New York University Press.

Gonzales, R. G. (2016). *Lives in limbo: Undocumented and coming of age in America*. Oakland: University of California Press.

Hernández-Truyol, B., Harris, A., & Valdés, F. (2015). Beyond the first decade: A forward-looking history of LatCrit theory, community and praxis. *Berkeley La Raza Law Journal, 17*, 169–216.

Kim, D. (2011). A young English learner's l2 literacy practice through dialogue journals. *Journal of Reading Education, 36*(3), 27–34.

Lopez, N. (2003). *Hopeful girls, troubled boys: Race and gender disparity in urban education*. New York, NY: Routledge.

Mayher, J. (1990). *Uncommon sense*. Portsmouth, NH: Boynton Cook.

Nassaji, H., & Cumming, A. (2000). What's in a ZPD? A case study of a young ESL student and teacher interacting through dialogue journals. *Language Teaching Research, 4*(2), 95–121.

Noblit, G. W., Flores, S. Y., & Murillo, E. G. Jr. (2004). *Postcritical ethnography: Reinscribing critique*. Cresskill, NJ: Hampton.

Noguera, P., Hurtado, A., & Fergus, E. (Eds.). (2013). *Invisible no more: Understanding the disenfranchisement of Latino men and boys*. New York, NY: Routledge.

Peregoy, S. F., & Boyle, O. (2017). *Reading, writing, and learning in ESL: A resource book for teaching K-12 English learners*. Boston, MA: Pearson.

Peyton, J. K., & Reed, L. (1990). *Dialogue journal writing with nonnative English speakers: A handbook for teachers.* Alexandria, VA: TESOL Press.

Ríos Vega., J. (2015). *Counterstorytelling narratives of Latino teenage boys: From Verguenza to Echale Ganas.* New York, NY: Peter Lang Publishing.

Ríos Vega, J., & Franeta, S. (2017). DREAMers in double exile: Teachers can be allies to LGBTQ students. In S. Wong, S. Sanchez Gosnell, A. M. Foerster Luu, & L. Dodson (Eds.), *Teachers as allies: Transformative practices for teaching DREAMers and undocumented students* (pp. 108–120). New York, NY: Teachers College Press.

Sáenz, V. B., & Ponjuan, L. (2009). The vanishing Latino male in higher education. *Journal of Hispanic Higher Education, 8*(1), 54–89.

Sáenz, V. B., Ponjuán, L., & López Figueroa, J. L. (2016) *Ensuring the success of Latino males in higher education. A national imperative.* Stylus Publishing.

Saldaña, J., & Omasta, M. (2018). *Qualitative research: Analyzing life.* Thousand Oaks, CA: SAGE.

Sánchez, B., Colón, Y., & Esparza, P. (2005). The role of sense of school belonging and gender in the academic adjustment of Latino adolescents. *Journal of Youth and Adolescence, 34*(6), 619–628.

Saunders, M., & Serna, I. (2004). Making college happen: The college experiences of first-generation Latino students. *Journal of Hispanic Higher Education, 3*(2), 146–163.

Solórzano, D., & Yosso, T. J. (2009). Critical race methodology: Counter-storytelling as an analytical framework for educational research. In E. Taylor, D. Gillborn, & G. Ladson-Billings (Eds.), *Foundations of critical race theory in education* (pp. 130–147). New York, NY: Routledge.

Staton, J., Shuy, R. W., Peyton, J. K., & Reed, L. (1988). *Dialogue journal communication: Classroom, linguistic, social and cognitive views.* Norwood, NJ: Ablex.

Stefancic, J. (1998). Latino and Latina critical theory: An annotated bibliography. *La Raza Law Journal, 10,* 423–498.

Taylor, E. (2009). The foundation of critical race theory in education: An introduction. In E. Taylor, D. Gillborn, & G. Ladson-Billings (Eds.), *Foundations of critical race theory in education* (pp. 1–13, 130–147). New York, NY: Routledge.

Torres, M., & Fergus, E. (2012). Social mobility and the complex status of Latino males: Education, employment, and incarceration patterns from 2000–2009. In. P. Noguera, A. Hurtado, & E. Fergus (Eds.), *Invisible no more: Understanding the disenfranchisement of Latino men and boys* (pp. 19–40). New York, NY: Routledge.

Valenzuela, A. (1999). *Subtractive schooling: U.S.-Mexican youth and the politics of caring.* Albany, NY: Sunny Press.

Vigil, J. D. (2012). Street socialization and the psychosocial moratorium. In P. Noguera, A. Hurtado, & E. Fergus (Eds.), *Invisible no more: Understanding the disenfranchisement of Latino men and boys* (pp. 279–288). New York, NY: Routledge.

Vygotsky, L. (1978). *Mind in society.* Cambridge, MA: Harvard University Press.

Yosso, T. J., Smith, W. A., Ceja, M., & Solórzano, D. G. (2009). Critical race theory, racial microaggressions, and campus racial climate for Latina/o undergraduates. *Harvard Educational Review, 79*(4), 659–690.

CHAPTER TWO

(Im)migration Journey

From Honduras to the U.S.A.

First, I want to tell you how difficult it was to come from my country to here. I am going to write about my life on my way to get a better education and to meet my father. When I left my country, I was 13 years old. It was difficult and hard for me because while I was with my cousin back home, I felt so lonely. One of the most difficult things was to cross borders. I remember that at the first border, we hid from the cops in the forest. We found bad people on our way and a couple of them were good. The bad people just thought about money and the good people thought about helping us. When I passed the Guatemalan border, it was midnight. You could clearly hear the wolf howling. I was scared because I thought that I will die, but God was with me. He gave me the strength to tolerate all those stuffs. Sometimes, I wanted to back with my grandma. I prayed to God for my life. Sometimes I thought like a lot of people will never make it, and I would never be able to see my Dad. We stopped at a lot of places where poor people helped and sold food. Most of the times, I was on the train, that was terrible because it had a bad smell like if something was dying.

One day we were on the train and minutes after it stopped, it was very hot. I could remember that all men were not wearing shirts. Then, when we saw people running. They closed the door, but the door did not close. Also, they tried and tried a lot of times; however, they tried to close it. The door was close like one hour, and we could not make any more noise because the police would find us. So, we remained quiet. We were dehydrating and we couldn't stand the heat. An hour later, we didn't hear any sound, so people opened a little the door and didn't see anybody. Then, the train started running again. When I crossed the river in Mexico, it was so cold, it was frozen. Then the man who came with us asked if we had dark clothes. We had to wear them because if we didn't, we would only have another chance to pass but without clothes.

When we passed the river, we were cold. We hugged each other to keep ourselves warm. No matter with whom you were, but that was the only thing for you to keep yourself safe and warm. Then, we walked three days and four nights. My feet were dirty and in pain. A lot of people died in those days. Thanks to God because we had money in our pockets. Sometimes, I gave others in the group some money for them to buy some food, so they could eat. I am so sorry for them because they tried but they couldn't make it. I am so glad that I am still alive because God gave me all the strength to make it. The man who brought us left us at the border of Mexico because he needed to go back to Honduras.

It was on December 6th that I got to the Mexico-U.S.A. border. We stayed like two weeks in a house. There were good people that paid for staying in their house. One week later, we decided that we wanted to cross the border, but during that time it was so dangerous. The old man told us that if we wanted to come to our country, we can leave their house and try it. My cousin and I were scared so we waited until everything was calm. Other people passed, but unfortunately, the cops caught them and sent them back to their country.

After three days, they told us that everything was ready. We took our clothes and got ready to leave. After two days walking in the forest, we felt someone was looking for us. We ran away, but we were separated. I took the opposite way that my cousin did. My group was hiding thinking that my cousin had taken the train that night.

In the morning, we took another train. I remember that one of the wagons had cars. We got inside them and got some sleep. Hours later, we woke up and the cops were checking the train, so we stayed there, but we had to be really quiet, especially if the door of the wagon was open. Unfortunately, the cops found us and took us to jail. They asked all for our names and where we were from. I told them that I was from San Luis Potosi, México.

After asking me a lot of questions about Mexico, they gave me food and clothes to wear. It was around 12:00 a.m. when they took me to Mexico Plaza. I called the old man and two days later, I saw my cousin again. We didn't have any problems. Finally, after that, we took two buses to get to Houston. Then we took a van. After a few hours, I came here to North Carolina and I never saw my cousin again. (Katie's journal)

Introduction

Writing about (im)migration usually was like a healing process for many of my former English as a second language (ESL) students. It not only allowed them to express their stories of sacrifice and hope, but it also let me learn about their personal lives. I always related Katie's story to the book *Enrique's Journey* by Sonia Nazario (2014), where she narrates the story of a Honduran boy who decided to come to the U.S. to reunite with his mother. Like Enrique, Katie's journey pushes her to leave her relatives behind to reunite with her father in North Carolina. Her stories talk about her journey from Honduras, Guatemala, and México. When she wrote this entry, her parents were no longer together. Her mom was living in the United States, but in a different state. Katie had a closer relationship with her father. She always showed an amazing and positive attitude toward life. Although she went through a lot back in her homeland and then her immigration journey, she was very polite and always felt optimistic about her education.

In this chapter, I use the participants' journal entries to document their painful immigration journeys to the U.S. I analyze how most of them were left behind by their parents when they were still infants and how they reunited with their parents, who some of them saw as strangers. Others had to relearn how to refer to their biological parents since the only parents they were used to were their grandparents. Additionally, this chapter includes the narratives of three Caribbean Latinx students and their experiences adapting to the American school system. Elisa and Santiago share about their experiences with issues of language, race/ethnicity intersect language discrimination and racism. Mauricio's narratives talk about how his parents decided to send him to live with a relative after experiencing with drug gangs back on Puerto Rico. Although these participants encountered multiple personal and social hurdles in school, homes, and the community, they share how their parents' support allowed them to remain in high school and graduate.

Border Crossers

Living in Trump's era and his anti-immigrant policies toward Mexican and other Latin American individuals is not new to those who have had no choice but to risk their lives to come to the United States, looking for better opportunities, education, or running away from gangs and violence. The stories shared in this chapter are full of sadness, uncertainty, pain, and hope. While most immigrant and undocumented individuals arrive to this country at early age, many of them do not have memories from their childhood before they came to this country. What is important to highlight in this book is the fact that all of the participants arrived when they were teenagers, so they do have a strong frame of reference about their childhood experiences before reuniting with their parents or relatives. All of the participants' stories show a second departure experience from their loved ones. First, when their parents left their homelands to pursue better jobs and opportunities for their loved ones (Portes & Rumbaut, 2001). Second, when these teenagers leave their homelands, leaving grandparents and relatives behind to join their parents. This chapter will explain how those (im)migration journeys shaped the participants' lives as they decided to either cross borders illegally to join their parents and relatives or those who came here legally but who experience the same layers of oppression and marginalization that most Latinx students go through in this country.

Never Give in

When I left my country, I had to sacrifice many things that you never forget because it's part of your life. I know many Latinos sacrifice many things to move to the U.S. It's a very difficult situation because time is longer day after day. When I immigrated to the U.S., I cried many times because I sometimes missed important things in my life, but it helped me to continue working toward my goal. It's like that main factor is telling me why I have to work hard. Family is the most important factor since everybody wants you to be successful. Also, I left my country to be close to my mother. I used to miss her a lot. She was in the U.S. before I came here. (Francisco's journal)

Similar to Katie's journey, Francisco's journal entry talks about his experience once in the United States. It talks about his sacrifice while leaving his relatives behind but his goal to reunite with his mom who was already living and working in this country. His mother left him with his grandmother when he was five years old (Garcia, 2001; Gonzales, 2016; Suárez-Orozco and Suárez-Orozco, 2001). After 11 years, Francisco's mother decided to pay a *coyote* (smuggler) to bring him to the United States without legal documentation. He recounts,

Vine caminando por la frontera. De Veracruz salí a la ciudad de México, de México a la frontera de Sonora y de ahí para acá caminando. Cruzamos con un coyote y un grupo de personas. Mi mamá pagó el coyote. En ese entonces creo que pagó como 4,000 por cada uno.

I walked through the border. From Veracruz, I traveled to Mexico City, from Mexico City to the Sonoran border, and then walked all the way up to here. We crossed with a smuggler and a group of people. My mom paid a smuggler. Back then, I think she paid like 4,000 per each of us.

Juan Ríos: Dicen que la gente ya debe dinero antes de llegar aquí.

Juan Ríos: People say that immigrants already owe money even before they get here.

F: Si, lo que pasa es como funciona, bueno en México la gente que viene para acá pide dinero porque le tienes que dar al coyote enseguida llegas aquí, pagas cuando la persona está aquí. Ya consiguen el dinero y la persona que le presta es usualmente una persona que está aquí. Al menos que tu tengas un familiar, un papá que pague por ti. Y ya cuando llegan aquí, es por eso dicen que ya llegando aquí ya tienes una deuda que tienes que pagar para atrás al que te prestó. En el caso de personas adultas sería así. Pero uno si te pagan tus papás, uno si sabe lo que está pasando a los 16 años, pero está un poco confundido.

F: Yes, what happens is the way it works. Well, in Mexico people who decide to come here borrow money because they have to pay a smuggler once they get here. They pay when the person is here. They get the money and the person who lends the money is already here (in the U.S.) unless they have a relative, a parent that can pay for them. And when they get here, that's why they say that once you get here, you already have debts. They have to pay back to those who lent them the money.

Francisco's journey was probably easier compared to his new challenges once in this country (Cammarota, 2008; Gándara & Contreras, 2009). Although he was always a quiet and mature teenager, he experienced problems with the language and since he was 16, he was registered as a high school freshman student. He could not speak English fluently, but his willingness to learn and to study was usually shown through his writing skills. When he was my student, I asked him to write about his first experience in North Carolina.

Moving to North Carolina

I moved to North Carolina four years ago. It was the hardest time because I didn't have any idea how the United States was. I had my mother here and some relatives. I didn't speak the language. I always needed somebody to translate for me. It was uncomfortable. The buildings were entirely different. I felt as a new world. I felt a new beginning where I had to survive for the first months. I was always at home because my mother worked Monday through Friday and my brother went to school.

Francisco wanted to support his mother financially (Cammarota, 2008). Antonio, his brother, did not cross the border at the same time and never told his mother that he was coming to the United States. It was his grandmother who paid the "coyote." She sent him with a relative when he was 11 years. He said,

Yo crucé ilegalmente por la frontera de Arizona. Fue sin mi madre saber porque ella no quería que nosotros corriéramos ese riesgo de venir ya que éramos menores de edad y teníamos una corta edad para venir para acá. Al yo cruzar me tardé cuatro días. Mi mamá no se enteró hasta dos días antes que yo pisara Estados Unidos.

I crossed illegally through the Arizona border. I came here without telling my mom since she did not want us to risk our lives to come here because we were minors and very young to come here. It took me four days to cross (the border). My Mom knew about it two days before I arrived in the United States.

Once Antonio reunited with his mother, she registered him in middle school since she did not want him to work. Antonio's personality was opposite than Francisco. While Francisco was always quiet and reflective, Antonio was more outgoing and opinionated. By the time he was my student, although I never asked him about his sexual orientation, I realized he was different and how some of Latino male students made comments about his mannerisms.

Similarly, to Francisco's and Antonio's immigration journey, Dulce immigrated from Veracruz, México without legal documentation. Along with her younger sister, her parents paid a *coyote* (smuggler) to cross the border. Her parents had been living in the United States for two years after they decided to bring them. She said,

> Bueno, mis papás tomaron la decisión. Ya ellos vivían aquí y mandaron a buscar a mi hermana y a mí. Nosotros vivíamos con unas tías y de repente sólo nos dijeron, "Se van con sus papás." Y tuvimos que agarrar un autobús que nos llevó hasta la frontera. En la frontera llegamos a una casa donde esperamos alrededor de dos días para que nos cruzara el coyote.

> *Well, my parents decided since they were already living here … and brought my sister and me. We used to live with our aunts and all of sudden, they just told us "you will join your parents." We had to take a bus that dropped us off by the border. At the border, we stayed in a house for two days while we waited around two days to be crossed by a smuggler.*

It was not until I read about my students' immigration journey when I realized how vulnerable minors are while crossing the borders with strangers. This was when I heard their stories about how other people become victims of robbery or sexual assault while coming to the United States.

Julio was born in Córdoba, México. Like the previous participants, Julio's parents moved to the United States before they decided to bring him to join them. While his parents were in the United States, Julio was raised by his grandmother and attended a Catholic (private) school in his homeland. Although Julio came to this country without legal documentation, his immigration journey differs from his comrades since he came by plane but with somebody else's passport. He was four when his parents moved to the United States. Then four years later, his mom went back to México to bring him to the United States. He shared,

> Two years later, by this time, I was like when my Dad left, I was three years old. A year later, my Mom leaves. He starts working and sends money to go for my Mom. My Mom leaves and I stayed with my grandma. The plan was that they wanned to be stable, find a place and all those things, so they will get some money and then get for me. My Mom meets all these people from church; I don't remember the name of the church, Pentecostal, I guess, so she started meeting all these people and there is this lady there and she has two kids and she said, "I have to get for my two kids and then." I don't know if you knew, but back then for the kids you didn't have a picture in their passports, so this lady was, "I go, pick up your kid and make him pass like he's mine." My mom came to Mexico with that lady and I left. And that's how I ended up going to the US. I crossed the border with papers, but they were not mine. It was a real passport, but it wasn't my name.

> My mother crossed the border two times. That's why I love my mother so much 'cause I remember her telling me like, "I told your Dad and he told me why you don't go, get him and come back" and he was like "Hell no, I will not cross the border again." So, my mom, being a woman, she said, "If you are not gonna do it, I will do it." She packed her

things. She came. She saw her family. She brought my sister and we left. She crossed the border illegally again and I crossed the border but on a plane. My mother crossed the border with all the illegal people. I came on the plane with her friend.

Border crossing stories, especially from Central American countries are even more painful and challenging. When I met Diana, Sofia, and Esperanza, I never thought how difficult it would be to cross not only one but two or three borders before coming to this country. Through their oral and written narratives, I learned about leaving grandmothers, who they used to call Mom, behind. I learned about being vulnerable for being a minor and female. Additionally, I learned about meeting parents for the very first time after many years, and who now felt like strangers. And I also learned about conflicts with relatives once they were in this country. It is important to highlight that my students arrived in this country when they were either pre-teenagers or teenagers, so they and their relatives had to endure adolescence and identity issues (Behnke et al., 2010; Brewster & Bowen, 2004; De Genova & Ramos-Ayala, 2003).

Diana, who came from Choluteca, Honduras, shared how her parents lied to her when she first came to North Carolina. She said,

> Prácticamente mis papás me trajeron engañada porque según solamente venía por dos años. Cuando cumplí los dos años de hecho yo les recordé de que ellos me habían dicho de que yo solo iba a venir aquí por dos años, aprender el idioma y eso era todo y ya que me regresaran para mi país porque yo extrañaba mucho a mi abuela, que era la que yo ví como mi papá y como mi mamá. Mis papás se vinieron antes. Creo que mi papá se vino en el 1991 y mi mamá se vino en el 1992. Yo llegué aquí en el 2002.

> *Practically, my parents lied to me because according to them, I was only coming for two years. When the two years passed by, I reminded them what they had promised me to be here for only two years, learn the language and that was it, and be back to my country, because I missed my grandmother a lot, who was the person I saw as my father and mother since my parents left before. I think my father came in 1991 and my mom in 1992. I came here in 2002.*

When Diana was in my class, she was always quiet and reluctant to speak in English. She was very concerned about being ridiculed or made fun of due to her lack of fluency and accent the new language. I also discovered that Diana's parents were pastors at a Latino Christian church. I never knew how her parents controlled her life until after I reunited with Diana to write this book. I always noticed that Diana wore long skirts and did not participate in any extracurricular activity after school. Instead, she helped her parents at home and at their church. During our interview, Diana mentioned how her parents paid a *coyote* (smuggler) to bring her to the United States. She shared,

Soy del sur de Honduras. Soy de Choluteca, hace fronteras con Guatemala, Nicaragua, El Salvador. Vine por tierra, cruzando fronteras. Crucé El Salvador, Guatemala y México. Demoré 11 días. Vine con un coyote.

I am from the southern side of Honduras. I am from Choluteca, which borders Guatemala, Nicaragua, and El Salvador. I came here by land, crossing borders. I crossed El Salvador, Guatemala, and Mexico. It took me 11 days. I came with a smuggler.

Diana did not like the idea of living in the United States for good. She was used to her grandmother, who she referred as her real mom. When she came to live with her parents, it was very hard since they were not used to her neither was, she. Similar to Diana's journey, Sofia came from El Salvador. Her parents left her country when she was 3 years of age. Since then her grandparents raised her after her grandfather passed away due to an accident. When she was 14, her parents decided to bring her to the United States without legal papers. She shared,

El coyote era de México pero estaba viviendo en El Salvador. Ya cuando le dieron la noticia a la abuela, la abuela se impactó mucho, no quería que me viniera pero yo tenía esa curiosidad de conocer a mis papás. Tenía un hermano, sabía que mi mamá estaba embarazada, que iba a tener otro niño, so yo quise venirme para conocerlos este y pues me vine, me tarde un día en cruzar la frontera de El Salvador a Guatemala porque no tenia la mayoria de edad y no tenía a mis padres para poder cruzar la frontera legalmente entre El Salvador y Guatemala. Entonces, me la pasé de mojada también de El Salvador hasta Guatemala. Luego eso fue en un día. Luego de Guatemala para México, duramos casi dos meses para cruzar de Guatemala a México porque hicimos dos intentos de cruzarlos y no se podía. Entonces nos regresamos porque nos decían estaba muy peligroso; porque había muchas pandillas, mucha delincuencia. Decían que ellos mismos le pedían dinero a los coyotes para poderte dejar cruzar al otro lado. En ese entonces siempre nos quedamos en un río y nos regresábamos y nos decían que no. La persona que iba conmigo era una novia de mi abuelo, supuestamente ella me iba ir cuidando en el camino pero cuando ella miró que era muy difícil de cruzar de Guatemala a México, ella decidió regresarse, so de Guatemala para México yo estaba sola. Pero lo bueno es que el coyote sí fue bueno. El siempre me mantuvo con los de menores edad. Se llevó a su novia para que ella siempre estuviera con nosotros. Tardamos como dos meses para cruzar para México. Luego de México para Chicago pienso que fue menos. Fue como semanas. Ya cruzamos para acá. Pero de México a Chicago, caminamos una noche entera. Cuando llegamos al otro lado para ya los Estados Unidos estaba un camión y ya nos estaba esperando para subirnos. Y ya nos subimos y el señor iba muy nervioso porque el carro donde nos llevaba a nosotros lo habían implementado a que fuera en medio de dos; había uno atrás y uno al frente y en el medio era donde íbamos nosotros. No nos movían por grupos grandes. Éramos grupos pequeños como de seis, ocho pero ellos lo hacían así porque no querían que ningún otro carro se le pegara a donde iban las personas. Era un *pick-up*. Entonces las personas que iban acostadas allí les habían puesto como una carpet arriba a ellos para que no se pudiera ver que eran personas que iban atrás. La persona que iba manejando se puso muy nerviosa y se le pegó una *state trooper* y se puso muy nervioso, perdió el control del carro, fuimos como a un cerco y en ese cerco él gritó, "Corran, sálganse", y pues abrieron las puertas y empezamos todos a correr. Corrimos el cerco. Luego nos metimos a un bosque. Luego de ese bosque, allí estuvimos esperando porque andaba un airplane andaba arriba chequeándonos. Eso duró como por dos horas. Eso fue ya en Estados Unidos. Creo que en Chicago. Ya cuando estábamos allí, el (coyote) empezó a hacer llamadas. Empezó a describir el lugar donde estábamos, el lugar donde se había quedado el carro. Ya como a las tres horas nos fueron a recoger y después de eso nos llevaron creo que era como una trailer. Nos tenían con mucha gente. Cuando yo llegué había mucha gente, si muchos otros hispanos que venían de Centro América, de México, de todos lados. Ya de allí, los coyotes se contactó con mis papás, le pidió que le diera lo que restaba, que les quedaba para ellos poderme mandar para aquí Norte Carolina y mis papás le depositaron el dinero y ya ellos me mandaron en una van. Me mandaron, me recuerdo que el lugar donde me fueron a dejar era en frente de McDonald's, en la gasolinera. En una gasolinera me fueron a dejar y ya hasta ahí fue cuando conocí a mis papás y a mi hermano, que en ese tiempo él tenía ocho años.

The smuggler was from Mexico but was living in El Salvador. When they (her parents) told the news to my grandmother, she was in shock since she did not want me to come, but I was curious about meeting my parents; I had a brother, I knew my mother was pregnant, that she was going to have a new child, so I wanted to come, to know them. It took me one day to cross the border from El Salvador to Guatemala because I was still a minor and did not have my parents to cross the border legally between El Salvador and Guatemala. Then I crossed illegally from El Salvador to Guatemala. Then it took a day. Then from Guatemala to Mexico, it took us almost two months to cross from Guatemala to Mexico because it was very dangerous, because there were a lot of gangs, a lot of delinquency. People said that gang members asked smugglers for money to let us cross the border. Back then, we always stayed by the river and then came back to cross but were always told that we could not do it. The person who came with me was my grandfather's girlfriend. She was supposed to take care of me on my way, but when she realized how difficult it was to cross from Guatemala to Mexico, she decided to go back, so from Guatemala to Mexico, so I was by myself. But the good thing was that the smuggler was nice. He always kept me with other minors. He took his girlfriend, so she could be with us all the time. It took us two months to cross to Mexico. Then from Mexico to Chicago, I thought it was a month, or weeks to cross. From Mexico to Chicago, we walked, we walked a whole night. When we crossed to the other side in the United States, there was a truck waiting for us to get in. When we got in, the driver was very nervous because the plan was that our truck would be in between two other cars, one in the front and the other in the back. They (smugglers) did not take us in large groups. We were small groups like six, eight, but they did it like that because they did not want any other vehicle to get closer to us. It was a pick-up truck, people were laid down with a carpet on top, so nobody could see they were people. The driver was very nervous when a state trooper got closer; he lost control of the truck, we ended up in an empty lot and in that lot, he shouted, "run, get out of the truck", and then people opened the doors and all of us started running, we ran throughout the empty lot, then we got into the woods. Then in the woods, we waited since there was an airplane searching.

It lasted like two hours. It was already in the United States. I think it was in Chicago. Once we were here, he (the smuggler) started making phone calls. He started describing the place where we were, the place where the truck was. Within three hours, people came to pick us up and then they took us to a trailer. We kept us with a lot of people. When I came, there were a lot of people, yes, a lot of Hispanics who came from Central America, from Mexico, from everywhere. From then, the smugglers contacted my parents. They asked my parents for the rest of the money, so they could send me to North Carolina and my parents deposited the money and then they sent me on a van. They sent me; I recall that the place where they left me was across from McDonald's at the gas station. They left me at the gas station and then it was when I met my parents and my brother, who by that time was eight years old.

Out of all of my students' experiences as a high school teacher, the one that impacted me the most was about Esperanza. Esperanza is an indigenous Mayan girl from Guatemala, whose first language is *Acateco* (Akatek). When she came to my classroom, I noticed something was not right in Esperanza. She could hardly speak Spanish. Instead, she was always quiet. Her foster mother, a White middle class and religious leader woman and I developed a very strong relationship. I was told that I could not ask Esperanza many questions about her life in the United States. I felt like Esperanza's *padrino* (Godfather) at school. I knew Esperanza had something that made her very vulnerable but special at the same time. When I started collecting data for this book, Esperanza knew I was in town. She contacted me and volunteered to be part of my project. While analyzing Esperanza's data, I realized that she never told exactly how she traveled from Guatemala to the United States. After having a long conversation with her, she shared with me how painful it was to recall how she made it to this country. She wrote,

When I left Guatemala to come to the U.S., I was 14 years old. A "coyote" picked me up. I remembered we went through different cities in Guatemala. We drove in the car for one day. When I came to the border line with other people, they were attacked by some thieves. I was lucky since I could hide between bushes, so the thieves couldn't spot me. I saw the thieves beating up people and taking their money. The same night, I started walking along with the other people. We walked all night in the desert. I carried a bag and a gallon of water with one pair of jeans. It was hot, about 108 degrees. I witnessed so many things like dead people's bones, snakes, and wild animals running around like wolves and horses. I only walked at night because it was easier that way, so immigration people couldn't spot me. I had to be quiet walking at night. I walked for 65 days. At the end of the desert, another "coyote" picked me up and brought me to Arizona. At this new place, I stayed for 3 days until the "coyote" communicated with another "coyote" who brought us to our families in the U.S. come to a city and join other people who were coming to the U.S. too. From this city, that's where we began to walk for one night and one day through the woods. We were in the woods for 5 days. I remembered one morning when a truck picked us up. There were a lot of people in this big truck and everyone was standing up. It stank so bad. There were little kids along with us. This truck took us somewhere in Mexico. It was at a huge house where we could rest and have some food. Then after another truck picked us up with the same people in it. There was no air. I was holding on someone's waist because the truck was very high. This truck took us to another city in Mexico. From this city, I took a bus to get to the Mexican border and spent the night in another house. While I was waiting for the truck to take me to the border line to cross, I was picked by a truck at noon because it was better to cross the desert at night, so the immigration patrols could not spot me.

Esperanza's experience was filled with many challenges. In two instances, I noticed that she tried to cut her wrists, like trying to kill herself. I immediately got in touch with her foster mother. Also, I had to protect her even more once I noticed how she was bullied because she looked Hispanic/Latina but was not able to communicate in either Spanish or English. Portes and Rumbaut (2001) claim that "People whose ethnic, racial, or other social markers place them in a minority status in their group or community are more likely to be self-conscious of those characteristics" (p. 151). I will address this situation later in the book. Coming to the United States was just the beginning of Esperanza's journey in her new country since she also became a victimized by one of her relatives.

> *I lived with a distant cousin and when I was living with him, I went through a lot and I could say he was abusive ... and I ran away because I could not handle what I was going through here in (name of the town). I ran away. I went to this house and knocked on the door and asked for help. I was so afraid because he was chasing me and that time that person called the police and I was taken to the hospital and he was taken to the jail and the hospital called. I guess the foster system care. Yes, yes DSS. Social services picked me up at the hospital and put me on a foster care, like a different one until they found someone who spoke Spanish and I awake to look for someone who spoke Spanish so they found my foster mom now ... I was taken to her house in 2011. I think ... yes, and that's how I got here. She was the one who brought me to (high school name). Yeah, I couldn't talk about for a long time, but now since I am older, yeah, I can talk about it. Yes, it was pretty hard, but is still hard. That's why, that's how I got to (high school name).*

Juan Ríos: Who brought you to school?
Esperanza: *I was in foster care and they almost put me on homeschooling, but the government said if you are in foster care you cannot be on home school, so my social worker had to figure out where I was going to do. They were going to do with me because I didn't speak any English, so they went through a lot of paperwork. They were afraid to put me in public school because of that barrier of English and not knowing anybody and then my social worker, they put me into public school.*

Sharing the same cultural background and heritage language with my students helped me to make strong bonds and connectedness. The ESL classroom became like most of my students said, *a familia*. There were times when I shared my personal testimonials as a Latino and immigrant man in the South. I told my students when the police stopped me or when I was stereotyped by locals as an undocumented Mexican for being brown-skinned and having a Spanish accent while speaking English. I recall when I asked my students to write their own "I Remember" poem as a self-reflection of their lives back in their countries and in the United States. I was surprised to know that Esperanza had kept hers after all of these years.

> I Remember
> I remember. I remember in Guatemala my family.
> They have a hard life.
> My father who doesn't have a job.
> My mom who sometimes cries because my father doesn't have a job.
>
> I remember. I remember the food in Guatemala is so different.
> I make tortillas for my father.
> He was happy and my mom too.
> I was happy to help my family although I am so young.
>
> I remember. I remember my friends in Guatemala.
> They were good friends.
> Sometimes I go to the mountains with them to play.
> One day, my Aunt invited me to go to the cemetery to watch gangs use cocaine.
>
> I remember. I remember my religion in Guatemala.
> All my family is Christian.
> Every Sunday I go to church with my family.
>
> I remember. I remember the school in Guatemala.
> It was different.
> All ages are together in the class.
> I went to school for three years in Guatemala.
>
> I remember. I remember in the desert it was scary because many people died coming to the United States.
> Many immigration police were passing at night.
>
> I remember. I remember my first day of school.
> My teacher gave me a paper in English.
> I couldn't read it.
> I answered the questions in Spanish.

I remember. I remember my first day her in the U.S.
I did not like the food.
The food here is so different because I never ate meat or drank soda before.

I remember. I remember the first time I saw a Black person.
I was looking for clothes at Walmart.
He scared me because I never saw a Black person before.

I remember. I remember I thought all White people did not know how to cook.
I thought they only ate in restaurants.
I remember, I remember.
Written by Esperanza. Taken from the journal.

Esperanza's writing skills in the ESL classroom allowed her to express her prior knowledge, immigration journey, and assumptions about unfamiliar things and people. She wrote about foods, people from other races and cultures, as well as places were totally new to her. It is evident that Esperanza's life back in Guatemala was very difficult. As her former teacher and scholar, I can understand why she had a hard time getting used to her new life in this country.

Leaving the Island(s)

While most Latinx studies address the experiences of Mexican and Central American students in the U.S., the stories of Caribbean Latinx are rarely analyzed by mainstream studies. Most of families from either Dominican Republic or Puerto Rico decided to move to the South due to family or friends' connections. Traditionally, immigrants from the Caribbean islands relocate in the Northern and Midwestern states (Flores-González, 2002; García Coll & Kerivan Marks, 2009; Lopez, 2003). However, I learned that some families find that in the South, the educational system is much better and crime level is lower than in other states. Elisa and Santiago came from the Dominican Republic at ages 15 and 14, respectively. Elisa said,

> We were supposed to move from the Dominican Republic to New Jersey. But the cost of living is very high in New Jersey and my father couldn't find any job. So, my Uncle was living here for about 13 years by then. He told my father to move here.

In the following chapter, I will explain more in-depth about Elisa's and Santiago's experiences in schools with issues of language, race/ethnicity, and higher education.

Mauricio's narrative might sound very common among teenagers. When I asked him why he came to live in the mainland since Puerto Rico is part of the United States territory (Commonwealth), he shared that his parents sent him to live with a relative after he was threatened by a gang member. During the interview, he shared that his goal was to go back to the island to talk to young people about his "lived" experiences. He said he wanted people to see him as a role model. Although, he never mentioned what he meant by lived experiences, he finally opened up and shared about the main reason why his parents sent him to live with a relative. He said,

> So, I mean from selling drugs or whatever. And that ended up that my best friend betrayed me because something that somebody said that I don't know how to say it in English. It is called *chotear* (snitch).

Mauricio shared with me how he used to sell drugs in his homeland. Once his parents knew about it and how he was threatened with a knife.

> Cuando yo tenía 15 años, yo vine de visita y tenía pasaje para volver pa' Puerto Rico, pero cuando ya era tiempo de irme de aquí para Puerto Rico, me dejaron aquí con mi prima primero. Cuando mi prima se mudó del apartamento para una casa, me mudé con ella.

> *When I was 15 years old, I came to visit and had a ticket to go back to Puerto Rico, but when it was time for me to go back to Puerto Rico, my parents left me here with my cousin first. When my cousin moved from her apartment to a house, I moved in with her.*

Mauricio's parents sent him to live with his relative avoiding him to join a gang or to end up selling drugs. He continued,

> Cuando le dijeron a ese supuesto amigo mío que yo le había "choteao" diciendo que él había vendido droga. Él fue donde mí. Allá cuando un maestro falta no tienes que ir a otra clase, te puedes quedar por la escuela caminando. Y yo estaba comprando una empanadilla y él me llamó a una esquina. Él me puso la cuchilla en las costillas y me estaba preguntando que si yo lo había choteado y entonces yo le estaba diciendo que no, pero en eso pasó un maestro y se fue. Y de allí me mudaron a otra escuela porque me di cuenta que lo que estaba haciendo era mal. Y ahí terminé el noveno grado, que es la intermedia. Y ahí me vine de vacaciones y ya después de ahí no volví pa' Puerto Rico.

> *When they were told that my supposed friend had said that I had snitched for selling drugs. He came to me. In Puerto Rico, when a teacher is absent, you do not have to go to a different class. You can leave and I was walking, I was buying an empanadilla and he called me on a street corner. He put a knife on my ribs and was asking me if I had snitched him and then I was telling him that no, but then a teacher passed by and he left. After that, my parents sent me to a different school because I realized that what I was doing was wrong. Then I finished*

ninth grade, which is middle school. And then vacation arrived and since then, I never have returned to Puerto Rico.

What Makes Me Proud

I have many things that make me proud. The most important one is what I have achieved. I'm proud of myself because I have achieved all of the things that one day, I thought they were going to be impossible. I learned the language in one year, I have been successful in school. I had stayed on the right track, and I'm more mature. I'm proud that I moved to this country because if I were in Puerto Rico, I couldn't achieve any of these things. I would had probably dropped out of high school and be doing bad things. Right now, I'm about to graduate from high school and go to college. I'm going to study automotive general technician and collision repair technician. Many people think that it is not a career and that anyone can do it. They also think it is a dirty job. To me it is a career and this not a dirty job. I'm proud that I'm going to be a technician, this is what I love. It is a humble job (Mauricio's journal entry).

When Mauricio wrote the above entry, he was a high school senior. Although he had all of his dreams to pursue higher education at a local community college, he found it very challenging and he decided to drop out (Gonzales, 2016). It is important to mention that Santiago became a naturalized citizen and Mauricio is an American citizen; however, their experiences in college were overwhelming. Mauricio thought he was asked to read long articles, which he did not enjoy doing. Santiago's experience was related to a lack of support by professors and college administrators. He shared how he felt invisible sometimes in the classroom (Gonzales, 2016). Elisa was the only one who resisted and learned to navigate higher education. Her tenacity and hardworking regardless her multiple challenges kept her in college until she transferred to a larger university to complete her college major in Fashion Design. The following section will discuss how the students found parental support to remain in school and to pursue higher education.

Parental Support

A Happy Time

The happiest time in my life was in the year 1999 because that year I saw my Dad for the second time in my life. He traveled to the U.S. when I was two to three years old, so by that time I did not know how he looked like, so when my mom told me that we were going to travel to North Carolina, I was so happy. When we arrived in the house, I saw three men standing outside the parking lot. I was so nervous, and my Mom told me to go hug my Dad, but I did not know who my Dad was, so when one of them say "Luz" I started to cry. My Dad looked so different like I had imagined him. (Luz's journal)

Luz's narrative was very common to me when I asked my students to write about their reunification with their parents after they were left behind. Some stories were filled with anger since some of my students did not understand why their parents had to leave them at an early age. Getting used to their biological parents was a challenge to many of my students.

Juan Ríos: ¿Cómo fue ese encuentro?

Sofía: Fue un poco raro en ese momento porque yo no sabia que sentir. Yo no sabía que estaba esperando de verlos a ellos.

Juan Ríos: How was that encounter?

Sofia: It was weird at that moment because I did not know what to feel. I did not know what to expect from them.

Sofia: Nunca los había mirado. Se sintió extraño el conocerlos, ya habían pasado muchos años. De tres años y medio a catorce, casi quince. Ya como que sentía ganas de conocerlos pero ya cuando los tuve al frente, fueron como que el si saber que son mis padres pero como el no sentir tanto excitement al verlos … este, me empezó a entrar mucha nostalgia por la abuela. Empecé a recordar cuánto quería a la abuela, que la había dejado sola. Pienso que al yo saber que ya estaba aquí, que ya estaba con mis papás, que estaba con mi hermano fue donde yo empecé a darme cuenta que yo había dejado a la abuela y me entró mucha nostalgia. Luego empezaba a llorar, a pedirles que me quería regresar. Que yo me quería regresar con mi abuela. Fue un cambio bien grande porque de estar viviendo solo con la abuela, luego con mis papás y mi hermano. Algo que yo quería cuando estaba en El Salvador, pero cuando ya estaba aquí, yo me quería regresar.

Sofia: I had never seen them. It was weird meeting them since many years had passed by. From three years and a half year to fourteen, almost fifteen. I wanted to meet them, but when I had them in front of me like knowing that they were my parents but not feeling so much excitement to see them. I started feeling nostalgic about my grandmother. I started remembering how much I loved my grandmother, that I had left by herself. I thought that knowing that I was already here that I had left my grandmother behind brought me a lot of nostalgia. Then I started crying. I asked my parents that I wanted to go back. That I wanted to be with my grandmother. It was a very huge change because from living with my grandmother, then with my parents and brother. It was something I wanted when I was in El Salvador, but once here, I wanted to go back.

JR: ¿Alguna vez reclamaste a tus papás porque te dejaron?

Sofia: A mi mamá. Al principio, al recién llegar porque yo hablaba por teléfono por la abuela y yo le decía mamá a la abuela y luego mi mamá pues se sentía como "la mamá soy yo."Y luego no sé, cuando estaba mas pequeña la abuela también decía que ella era mi mamá. Entonces ya entra eso como que te dicen que cuando estas pequeño que "tú mamá es la que te está criando no la que te engendró". Entonces es cuando empiezas a entender eso que te decían cuando estabas pequeño porque cuando estás pequeño te dicen muchas cosas y tú no las entiendes, pero cuando ya estas grande, tú analizas lo que te están diciendo. Ya cuando en ese tiempo que yo ya estaba aquí, yo empecé a analizar que sí, la que me había criado era la abuela y la que me había tenido era mi mamá pero no había estado conmigo todo ese tiempo. Entonces sí hubo mucha fricción. Nunca fui rebelde ni grosera, pero si me encerraba mucho. No conversaba con ellos y prefería muchas veces estar sola. No tenía eso mucho de querer convivir con ellos. Pienso que fue peor que haber sido rebelde porque a veces dicen que la rebeldía es como un llamado a que le prestes atención. Lo mio fue mas querer apartarme de ellos. Lo más difícil para ellos era que no me conocían. Yo tampoco los conocía. No saber cómo llegarme. Yo no saber cómo llegar con ellos. Fue muy difícil.

JR: Did you ever ask your parents why they left you behind?

Sofia: I asked my mom. At the beginning, when I came here because I used to talk to my grandmother and used to call my grandmother mom and then my mother felt like "I am your mother." And then I do not know, when I was little, my grandmother also said that she was my mom. Then you start thinking about those things you hear when you are little like, "your real mom is that one that raises you, not the one who birthed you." Then you start to understand what you were told when you were little because when you are little, you hear a lot of things that you do not really understand, but when you are an adult, you analyze that others are telling you. Once I was here, I started to analyze that yes, that my grandmother had raised and the one who birthed me was my mom, but she had never been with me all of this time. Then there was a lot of friction. I was never a rebel child nor rude, but I used to be closeted. I did not talk to my parents. I preferred to be by myself. I did not like to spend time with them. I think that it was even worse than being rebel because sometimes people say that being rebel is like a call, so others can pay attention to you. In my case, I wanted to stay away from them. The most difficult thing was that they did not know me. I did not know them either. They did not know how to approach me. It was very difficult.

Sofia's case was different since she decided to hide how much she missed her grandmother by isolating herself from her parents. Instead of being rebellious at home or school, she kept everything inside. However, she later on narrated how she developed panic attacks when started attending high school. Sofia was always a very respectful and hardworking student who pushed herself to learn English as soon as she could. During her interview she shared with me how bad she felt when she was taken out of the ESL courses. On the contrary, Diana's relationship with her parents was different than Sofia's. Her parents left Honduras when she was little, so she did not have a strong relationship with them. She shared how she had to make her parents believe how she missed and loved them.

JR: (Looking at her journal.) Cuenta acerca de lo que escribiste en el libro acerca de tu vida en Carolina del Norte. ¿Qué me puedes decir de eso?

Diana: Bueno, sí, como dice el libro sí estaba algo asustada.

Es que yo no conocía a mis padres. Yo tenía, comunicación con ellos solamente por teléfono. Y lo que yo hablaba con ellos era más lo que mi abuela me decía, que yo le dijera a ellos. Por ejemplo, darle una palabra de cariño, era mi abuela la que me ponía a hacerlo. No me nacía hacerlo porque yo no los conocía. Para mi ella (abuela) fue mi madre y fue mi padre.

JR: Tell me about what you wrote in your journal about your life in North Carolina. What can you tell me about it?

Diana: Well, like the book says that I was a little bit scared. I did not know my parents. I used to talk to them over the phone only. And what I talked to them was what my grandmother used to ask me to tell them. For example, when I told them a nice word, it was my grandmother who used to ask me to tell them. It was not on me to tell them a nice word because I did not know them. To me, my grandmother was my mother and father.

JR: ¿Cómo fue ese encuentro con tus papás?

Diana: Con mi papá, yo siento que tuvimos una conexión el instante en que nos vimos. Con mi mamá no, hasta el día de hoy no sé porque no.

JR: How was that encounter with your parents?

Diana: With my father, I think we had an instant connection when we saw each other. With my mother, no. Until today, I do not know why not.

Some of my students had a hard time learning school and social rules, usually seen as discriminatory and oppressive. Many of my students missed enjoying that freedom of hangout out late with friends or moving to places without being targeted or racially profiled as undocumented. Others shared with me how their parents did not allow them to start dating. It was very common to hear that some Latina students had run away from home. As they used to tell me, *Se la robaron* (she ran away with a man).

Juan Ríos: ¿Hoy en día que eres mamá, entiendes a tu mamá un poco mejor?

Juan Ríos: Now that you are a mother, do you understand your mother a little bit better?

Diana: (thinking very deep). Parte sí, pero muy poco. Creo que del hecho de que no crecí con ella. Era para que ella tomara una actitud diferente. Que se ganara mi confianza. Lo único que era reservada de decirle de manera de cómo yo me sentía al trato de ella. Nunca se lo he dejado saber.

JR: Now that you are a mother, do you understand your mom a little bit better?

Diana: A little bit. I think that I did not grow up near her. I think she should have taken a different attitude. She needed to develop my trust. I was very reserved to share the way I felt and how she treated me. I have never told her

JR: ¿Qué crees que era?

Diana: Creo que no se adaptaron a mi cambio. Yo llegué niña de allá. Aquí me torné adolescente, aquí me desarrollé como mujer. So, ese cambio en la naturaleza no supo cómo sobrellevarlo … ni yo tampoco porque era yo la que estaba cambiando. Era ella la que me tenía que aconsejar, "tienes que hacerlo de esta manera; no tienes que hacer esto porque va a pasar esto." Todo lo que aprendí, lo aprendí a golpes porque no tuve quien me instruya a cómo enfrentar ciertas situaciones.

JR: Why do you think that happened?

Diana: I think they did not get used to my change. I came as a girl here. Here, I became an adolescent, here I turned into a woman. So, that nature change, they did not know how to deal with. I did not either since I was the one changing. She was the one who needed to advise me, "You have to do it this way; You do not have to do that because that might happen." I learned all of those things the tough way because I never had someone who could guide me to face certain situations.

Other times I heard that families had decided to move to a different state or city, so my student stopped coming to school. Later I found out the student and his/her family were still living in town and that my student was working full-time in a factory or construction. Gándara and Contreras (2009) argue that low-income and minority parents do not usually have the cultural and social capital to access and to understand how the American system works. As a result, their children end up joining them in low-wage jobs, trapped in a cycle of poverty.

However, I also met supportive parents whose main goal was to make sure their children stay in school. A lot of my students were very appreciative about their parents' sacrifices to come to this country to find a better future for their children. One day, I asked my students to write about their role models and how they inspired them to do good in school. Francisco and Diana wrote in their journals.

My Role Model

Since I can remember I wanted to be like my Dad because he was very strong and smart. Even though he wasn't in Honduras with me, I always received his advice telling me that I have to respect adults and my family, who I used to live. When I got here, my Dad taught me that I have to go to church and give him my heart and my soul. My Dad not only one or two times told me that I have to study and make myself become somebody. My Dad is a smart person that everybody admires. He worries about other people. Now, he is a pastor and teaches people the word of God. He is my hero because he was the man that God chose to bring me here in the world. He also helps teach me how to behave. People love him because he helps them and worries about them. He doesn't care about if people love him or not, he only cares that he has to serve God.

Diana developed a closer relationship with her father than with her mother. It was like she never got along with her. By the time I interviewed Diana for this book project, she shared that her parents were no longer together after her mom realized her father was dating another mom from his church. I was also surprised to know that her father was no longer a pastor.

Parents' Jobs

I know my mother is my hero. She is a strong woman that supports their belongings like me. She went to work to give us a better lifestyle. We didn't have a father, but I have one because my mother did both jobs. I'm proud of her. She still works, but I promised myself that I will be somebody and she will not work for anybody anymore. She works in factories. I know it is hard because I can see how tired she gets when she returns home. The salary isn't that much either. She always tells me, "Don't stop studying because that's the only way that she can stop working." I like to study and will not stop. I want to work hard to become somebody and one day my mother will be proud of me. (Francisco's journal)

Francisco's sense of responsibility toward his mom's sacrifices instilled in him hard work through this education. Like I explained in the previous section, Francisco wanted to pursue high school back in México but it was not possible, so having the possibility to get a high school diploma in this country to be able to support his mother financially in the near future was his biggest motivation. Interestingly, Antonio's comments about his way to pay his mother back for her sacrifices were more related to pleasing her goal and become independent (Gonzales, 2016; Valenzuela, 1999). When I asked him who or what made him go to school every day, he responded,

Siempre quería darle (a la escuela) porque mi propósito siempre fue ser independiente. Entonces yo sabía que si yo le daba a mi mamá el diploma que ella esperaba de mí, podía irme tranquilo y empezar a independizarme y como que no tendría yo ese rechazo de ella al decir, "No acabaste, no me cumpliste." Era como una promesa que yo le debía a ella.

I always wanted to work hard (education) since my goal was always to be independent. Then I knew that if I gave my mother a high school diploma, that she expected from me, I could leave her house easily and to start being independent and that I would not be rejected by her

telling me, "You did not finish, you did not accomplish what you promised." It was like a
promise that I owed her.

Both Francisco and Antonio graduated from high school on the same year. Francisco continued working at a fast-food restaurant until he was laid off due to his lack of legal immigration documentation. Because of his age of arrival to this country, he could not benefit from Deferred Action for Childhood Arrivals (DACA) (I will talk about it in the next chapters). Antonio did receive DACA and moved away to a larger city in North Carolina, where he currently works on retail and does drag queen shows at local parties and gay clubs.

Santiago and Elisa had a very close relationship with their parents since they all came together from the Dominican Republic. I became a very good friend of Santiago's and Elisa's parents. One time I was teaching ESL classes to their father on Saturdays at a local community college. Also, on weekends I used to buy groceries at their uncle's grocery store. Also, Santiago's and Elisa's mother knew how much I enjoyed her spaghetti and famous drink *Morir Soñando*. Since Santiago and Elisa used to live in a different school district, they were supposed to attend a different high school. It was not until the writing of this book that I learned that their parents paid an extra tuition fee at my high school, so they could take my ESL classes. I felt so honored when they shared it with me. Medina and Macaya (2015) argues that the relocation of Latino/a families to the Southeast brought some challenges in schools, especially with unskilled teachers and counselors who were culturally sensitive or were able to speak Spanish.

When I asked my students to write about their treasures, Santiago decided to write about his parents as his biggest treasure.

> My treasures are my parents and my sister, they mean the world to me. God has blessed me with such great parents and sister. They are my treasure because they have always been there for me no matter what. My mom and dad have always helped me in everything, they have never had a "no" for me no matter what I have done. My sister is always there to help in anything. She also gives me advice. Even though we disagree a lot, I love her a lot. If something happens to them, I'll die.

It was clear that both Santiago and Elisa were very appreciative about their parents' sacrifices. Although both parents were not fluent in English nor do they have a college diplomas or well-paid jobs, they supported their children's education.

Juan Ríos: Did your family have something to do with it that you wanted to be somebody?
Elisa: Definitely, they always told me since I was little that I needed to go to the university, but it was all on me being in this country and how the Latino community has been discriminated … I definitely wanted to be the change.

Interestingly, Elisa was critically aware about how Latinx individuals are targeted in this country, but also, she wanted to accomplish her parents' goal and attend college.

> **Juan Ríos:** Did you support your parents when you worked at McDonald's?
> **Elisa:** No, because what my father did. He let the money so I could buy books and others like the gas. He supported me financially. They (parents) told us, "If you don't go to college, you are gonna be a nobody in this country". And we are for the minory ... (corrected herself) de la minoría (of the minority).and if you don't have an education, they (Americans) are gonna treat you like worst.

> Dear Alberto,
>
> This is my family. I took this picture of them because we love, and we try to help each other. Sometimes we help my father when he has to pay the bills. My mother takes care of my cousins sometimes. When she gets paid, she gives the money to my father to pay the bills. My sister says that when she finishes school, she will get a job to help my dad. My sister wants to go to college to get better opportunities for her and for us. Finally, if I finished high school, I will do the same. I would like to become a baseball player and I am planning to go back to my country just to visit my family and friends because there is a lot of violence. (Santiago's journal)

> **Juan Ríos:** Do you feel that in a certain way, they (her parents) sacrifice themselves for you to go to college?
> **Elisa:** Of course.
> **JR:** How did you finance your education?
> **Elisa:** At the beginning they paid for it until we found about financial aid ... for low income families ... because that's something I didn't know about it ... until somebody told me.
> **JR:** Did a counselor talk to you about FAFSA when you were in school?
> **Elisa:** Nope. I was in the second semester when I heard about it. I was a sophomore ... at RCC.

There is no doubt that my students' stories about (im)migration while coming to this country have shaped their lives with fear, uncertainty, and hope. Most of my students shared a second traumatic departure experience. First, when their parents left them behind under the custody of their grandparents or relatives. Second, when they had to leave their grandparents and relatives whom they used to see as their sole parents.

For those students, crossing borders was probably seen as an adventure or full of hope since they wanted to be with their parents after so long. Since most of them were children when their parents left them, it was a different adjustment phase from both sides. Some of them had a hard time calling and accepting their biological parents as their real parents. Others like Diana had a hard time getting along with her mother. Sofia preferred to be by herself while missing her grandmother whom she used to call Mom.

Attending school represented an outlet for most of these students. It was in school where they learned to support each other while not only learning the new language and culture, but to become resilient. The most amazing case was Esperanza's. It was through here education and sports where she could find her own voice with the support of her foster mother, teachers, and community members. I always knew Esperanza was going through a lot while she was my student; however, she did not feel ready to talk about her personal struggles until we reconnected years later, and she agreed to support my book project.

One of the most highlighting things that I would like to mention in this chapter is the students' parental support. Although most parents had no choice but to leave their children when they were still infants, they always stayed in touch with them by phone or some others like Julio's mother who went back to México to pick him up and send him on a plane with a fake passport and a woman from her church.

Once in the United States, parents preferred their children to attend school instead of getting them a job to support the family either here or relatives back home. Although many of my students in this book used to work part-time after school, they never abandoned their studies. Some others like Luz helped her mother to make and sell tamales until later during weekdays. Others worked at fast-food restaurants on weekends.

Summary

This chapter has explored the (im)migration journey of 12 of my former high school students. I have to confess that the first time I read their stories in their journals, I felt moved and since then I always saw my students as my heroes. I always thanked them for coming to school every day, ignoring that some of them were tired or worried about their relatives back home or having personal problems with their parents or in the community. Reuniting with my students to talk and to reflect about their experiences during and post-high school turned into a healing process for myself and them. The next chapter will analyze how my students experienced discrimination and racism in high school. In addition, it will discuss how a tracking system implemented in English language learners and low expectations from teachers, counselors, school administrators shaped my students' experiences in high school. Finally, it will analyze Julio's school to deportation pipeline.

References

Behnke, A. O., Gonzalez, L. M., & Cox, R. B. (2010). Latino students in new arrival states: Factors and services to prevent youth from dropping out. *Hispanic Journal of Behavioral Sciences, 32*(3), 385–409.

Brewster, A. B., & Bowen, G. L. (2004). Teacher support and the school engagement of Latino middle and high school students at risk of school failure. *Child and Adolescent Social Work Journal, 21*(1), 47–67.

Cammarota, J. (2008). *Sueños Americanos: Barrio youth negotiating social and cultural identities.* California: The University of Arizona Press.

De Genova, N., & Ramos-Zayas, A. Y. (2003). *Latino crossings: Mexicans, Puerto Ricans, and the politics of race and citizenship.* New York, NY: Routledge.

Flores-González, N. (2002). *School kids/street kids: Identity development in Latino students.* New York, NY: Teachers College Press.

Gándara, P. C., & Contreras, F. (2009). *The Latino education crisis: The consequences of failed social policies.* Cambridge, MA: Harvard University Press.

García Coll, C., & Marks, A. K. (2009). *Immigrant stories ethnicity and academics in middle childhood.* Oxford: Oxford University Press.

García, E. E. (2001). *Hispanic education in the United States: raíces y alas.* Lanham, MD: Rowman & Littlefield.

Gonzales, R. G. (2016). *Lives in limbo: Undocumented and coming of age in America.* Oakland: University of California Press.

Lopez, N. (2003). *Hopeful girls, troubled boys: Race and gender disparity in urban education.* New York, NY: Routledge.

Medina, Y., & Macaya Ángeles Donoso. (2015). *Latinas/os on the East Coast: A critical reader.* New York, NY: Peter Lang.

Nazario, S. (2014). *La travesía de Enrique.* New York: Random House.

Portes, A., & Rumbaut, R. G. (2001). *Legacies: The story of the immigrant second generation.* Berkeley: University of California Press.

Suárez-Orozco, C., & Suárez-Orozco, M. M. (2001). *Children of immigration.* Boston, MA: Harvard University Press.

Valenzuela, A. (1999). *Subtractive schooling: U.S.-Mexican youth and the politics of caring.* New York: State University of New York Press.

CHAPTER THREE

Navigating High School

The Day People Made My Family Feel Unwelcome

One day that my mother, my little sister, and I went to McDonald's, while my little sister was playing around with one of her friends that she had found there, at the other side of the fast food restaurant, there was a White woman eating her meal. My sister kept talking to her friend and joking around with her. The White lady turned around and said to my little sister "shut up." My mom got so mad that she was speechless. The only thing that she said was, *"Vieja grosera"* (old and rude woman) that lady didn't even understand what my mom just said to her, but she didn't care. She told my mother that if she didn't like the way things were in this country, then to go back from where she came from. Those words made me, and my family feel unwelcome, unwanted, and disrespected. That old lady kept running her mouth. I got really mad that I couldn't take her insults anymore, so I told her to shut the f*** up. That lady got so mad that she didn't even get to finish her food. She left say to us, "you are a bunch of stupid speaks." We didn't even pay attention to her, so we kept eating like nothing had happened. While she was walking out of the restaurant, some thoughts came to my head. I was thinking if people disrespect you why try to keep all your thoughts in your head when you can say them to them and make them feel the pain you feel with just a couple of words. (Julio's journal)

Introduction

Most of the students in this study shared experiencing discrimination and racism for multiple reasons. Julio's journal represents one of the multiple testimonials that I heard my students shared in class with unwelcoming individuals. Julio's frustration and sense of responsibility as the male figure at home encouraged him to advocate for his mom and sister. Based on his other journal entries and experiences with racist people led him to develop so much anger toward people who made him and his family feel like they did not belong to the U.S. (Yosso, Smith, Ceja, & Solórzano, 2009). In this chapter, I analyze how the participants narrate how discrimination and racism shaped their lives while they attended high school. They share how speaking their native language and their presence as Latinx were used as racial profiles to marginalize them. Additionally, I discuss how counselors' and teachers' low expectations lead these participants to become part of a tracking system that led them ill-prepared to become successful higher education candidates. Finally, contrary to many other studies about English as a second language (ESL) classes, I share how the participants' narratives about their experiences in the ESL classroom gave them a sense of *familia* where they could express their personal and familial challenges. Here, I discuss how the use of a culturally sensitive pedagogy (Gay, 2010; Villenas & Lucas, 2002) supported ESL and Latinx students.

Discrimination and Racism

Like Julio, Dulce also shared a similar racist incident when she felt being discriminated by one of her teachers for speaking in Spanish to her friend. She shared,

> Estaba otra amiga que recién había llegado, Carolina y pues ya yo entendía un poco más el inglés y le estaba explicando y la maestra dijo que no quería que habláramos español que era una clase para hablar puro inglés y que no quería escucharnos hablar español. Yo me molesté y le dije que no podía prohibirme hablar mi idioma.

> *I was with another friend that had just arrived, Carolina and then I understood a little bit of English and was trying to explain to her and the teacher told me that she did not want us to talk in Spanish that her class was to talk about everything in English and that she did not want to hear us talk in Spanish. I became very upset and told her that she could not ban me from speaking my language.*

I still recall Dulce's incident with her biology teacher, a long-term White woman with the reputation in the school and the community for being a great teacher; however, her attitude toward Latinx students speaking Spanish was evident. It was my first year at Ashes High School, so I took a lot time thinking about how to approach her concerning her comments to Dulce. It was in the teachers' lounge when I reminded her that she could not ban students to stop speaking their native language since it was their only way to support one another in her classroom. Unfortunately, there were other teachers with the same attitude about hearing another language, especially Spanish. Valenzuela (1999) claims that students feel alienated when teachers and students have different views about education. She adds, "Because teachers and administrators are better positioned than students to impose their perspectives, aesthetic caring comes to shape and sustain a subtractive logic" (p. 62).

Like Dulce, Luz also experienced discrimination for not being able to speak English when arrived in the U.S. Unfortunately, her teachers saw Luz as deficient since she could not do her homework or understand them. Instead of finding the resources to make her feel included and to be able to learn the target language, Luz was marginalized and punished for not turning in her homework.

> I came to North Carolina when I was almost nine years old. At first I did not like it and for more than five months I did not eat because I did not like the food and the only thing that I ate was fruit. My mom wanted to go back to Mexico because of me. I was getting sick and I started to lose a lot of weight. But my worst day was my first day at school I was so scared and more because in my class there was nobody that knew my language and whenever the teacher gave homework I never did it because I did not have anyone to help me at home. I remember that every day before going to school I started to cry because I did not want to go. (Dulce's journal)

During her interview, Luz recalled how she was punished for not being able to do her homework.

> Cuando llegamos eramos los únicos Latinos … y una de las partes más difíciles era que yo no entendía el idioma … y recuerdo que muchas veces tuve que estar en castigo por no hacer la tarea por motivo de no entender o no poder hablar el idioma.

> *When we arrived, we were the only Latinos and one of the most difficult parts was that I did not understand the language and I remember that I was punished many times for not doing my homework because I did not understand it or could not speak the language.*

> Juan Ríos: ¿Quién te castigaba?

> *Juan Ríos: Who punished you?*

> Luz: Mi maestra. Me ponía silent lunch. O no me dejaba ir a lonche con los otros estudiantes porque yo no tenía mi tarea. Entonces yo iba y agarraba mi comida y me iba pa' tras del salón por motivo de no hacer la tarea.

Luz: My teacher. She used to give me silent lunch or did not let me have lunch with other students since I did not have my homework. Then I used to get my food and went to the back of the room for not bringing my homework.

JR: ¿Pero no hacías la tarea por no hablar inglés?

JR: But you didn't do your homework because you did not speak English?

Luz: Por no saber pos yo tampoco sabía como leerlo y no tenía nadien en casa que me ayudara.

Luz: For not knowing since I did not know how to read it and did not have anyone at home who could help me.

JR: ¿Qué edad tenías?

JR: How old were you?

Luz: nueve. Estaba en cuarto y quinto porque yo llegué entrando a cuarto grado y ya después empecé el quinto.

Luz: Nine. I was in fourth and fifth grades. When I came here, I was placed in fourth grade and then I started fifth.

JR: ¿Y cómo empezaste hablar inglés entonces?

JR: And how did you start speaking English then?

Luz: …(took a deep breath) ahora is que por obligación tuve que aprender a fuerzas porque yo todos los días era un llanto porque … era como algo muy frustrante y yo llegaba con miedo porque yo no sabia como decir quiero ir al baño, quiero ir esto puedo tomar agua porque no sabía decirlo y una compañera que nunca voy a olvidar, que su nombre me ayudaba me ayudó y los días que ella faltaba pues era como un trauma para mi porque ella no estaba para ayudarme.

Luz: (took a deep breath) well, I had no choice. I had to learn the tough way because I used to cry every day. It was frustrating and I used to arrive to school frightened because I did not know how to say that I wanted to use the bathroom, I want this, I want to drink water. I did not know how to say those things. And a classmate that I will never forget; she used to help me. She helped me and when she missed school, well it was traumatic for me because she was not there to help me.

It is important to highlight that although these incidents took place when Luz first came to the U.S., she felt insecure about speaking English in front of others. I can recall when I used to remind her to practice her oral skills while talking to me; however, she refused to do it. She felt comfortable talking to me in Spanish.

Similarly, Julio shared how he felt discriminated for speaking English with a Spanish accent.

When I was in high school, I talked a little bit of English but didn't have a good accent, so my English was a Mexican English, you know. He told me, "Man you can't talk." The guy made fun of me all the time. So I was like. I don't like this kind of thing. That harassing and all that stuff, so I got in a fight at the JDRC.

Francisco also shared how he was bullied by a White student. He said,

Al principio la gente se burla de como hablas y todo, si intentas hacer algo. Una vez sí un alumno, yo estaba pidiendo algo a la maestra y se empezó a burlar, era un americano blanco, se reía, era así un poco como racista, no le caían bien los hispanos, porque él lo decía siempre. Decía que no deberíamos estar en la escuela si no sabíamos hablar inglés. Lo decía cuando no estaba la maestra.

At the beginning, people used to make fun of the way I spoke and everything, if I tried to do something. One day, a student, I was asking the teacher for something and he started to make fun of me. He was a White American. He laughed. He was like racist. He did not like Hispanics because he used to say it. He used to say that we should not be in school if we did not know how to speak English. He used to say that when the teacher was not around.

Whenever I asked my former students this last question, what they disliked the most about attending schools in the United States, it was usually about being segregated by mainstream classroom teachers and feeling invisible in the classroom for not being fluent in the new language. Antonio shared how he was once accused of hiding something that belonged to his math teacher and how his classmates blamed it on him. He could not defend himself due to the fact that he could not speak English. When I asked him if there, he experienced segregation at school, he agreed. He said,

Tal vez mucha segregación que tenían porque aunque no se notaba mucho, si la había. Por ejemplo, cuando una vez ellos me mandaron a la oficina simplemente porque yo no lo pude explicar muy bien a la maestra el problema del pizarrón. Ellos me mandaron a la oficina porque la maestra dijo que no estaba capacitada para estar en esa clase. Cuando yo llegué a esa oficina el principal me preguntó que me había pasado. Y yo solamente le dije que porque no podía resolver un problema y por eso la maestra me mandó a la oficina. Y de eso el principal dijo que ese era un problema que ella tenía que resolver y que iba a hablar y entrenar a los maestros para estar capacitados sobre esas situaciones, pero nunca pasó.

Maybe a lot of segregation that existed because even though it was not obvious, it still existed. For example, when one time, they (teachers) sent me to the office because I could not explain the problem written on the board to the teacher. They sent me to the office because the teacher said that she was not trained to teach that class. When I came to the office, the principal asked me what had happened. I told him that I could not solve a math problem and for that reason the teacher sent me to his office. And the principal said that it was a problem that she had to solve and that he was going to talk and train teachers to be more equipped when these things happen, but that never happened.

Juan Ríos: ¿En algún momento te sentiste segregado u oprimido por ser hispano?

Antonio: Sí. En la clase de computadoras. Yo era el único hispano que estaba en esa clase y ellos me sentaban hasta atrás ... y cada vez que yo preguntaba una pregunta o quería participar, ellos siempre me ignoraban.

Juan Ríos: Did you ever feel segregated or oppressed for being Hispanic?

Antonio: Yes. In the computer class. I was the only Hispanic in the class and they (teachers) asked me to sit in the back and every time I asked a question or wanted to participate, they always ignored me.

JR: ¿Quiénes te ignoraban?

Antonio: Los maestros y los alumnos porque normalmente teníamos trabajos en equipo ... y como que mi opinión nunca contaba, siempre la decía pero no estaba allí. Me sentía ignorado. Me sentía con ganas de no seguir en esa clase. Había veces que me dejaba de importar ... pero sabía que tenía que pasar esa clase para poder graduarme. Y eso era lo único que me mantenía ahí porque eso era lo que mi mamá quería, que yo me graduara.

JR: Who ignored you?

Antonio: The teachers and the students because usually we had to work as teams and like my opinion was never taken into account, like I was not there. I felt ignored. I felt like quitting that class. There were times when I did not even care, but I knew that I had to pass that class to graduate. And it was the only reason why I stayed there because it was what my mother wanted. She wanted me to graduate.

Like Antonio, Mauricio talked about being discriminated by a teacher just by being seen as Hispanic or Spanish speaker. He shared,

It was a math teacher, Mrs._____. I never understood her class. She was pretty tough, but whenever I asked for help, she never helped me, but she did help other people, so I failed her class.

Like Antonio, Elisa recalled how some teachers pushed her to talk in front of the class and being bullied by their English-speaking peers because of her Spanish accent in English. She also talked about feeling invisible to her teachers. Suárez-Orozco and Suárez-Orozco (2001) posit that many immigrant children who attend school are segregated and impoverished, making their transition to the new country more stressful. When I asked her about the least favorite thing about high school, she responded,

Well, when I used to ask some teachers. I know the language barrier. It was hard but I thought they didn't pay attention as I needed it. I felt I was invisible, the first time that I went to AHS. They knew I didn't know English and they asked me to be in front of everyone to present things that I didn't know how to explain or how to pronounce and a lot of kids laughed about me. I felt embarrassed because of the language.

It is important to highlight how Esperanza suffered prejudice and discrimination differently from other Latinx teenagers. Due to the fact that she started developing her English faster than her Spanish, she was usually targeted as one who wanted to become White. What most of her Latinx peers ignored was that Esperanza's first language was a Mesoamerican language of Guatemala, not Spanish (Arriaza, 2004; Kozol, 2012; Menjívar, 2002; Urrieta, 2003). She shared,

> When I realize now that I speak Spanish and English now. I feel like I was discriminated because a lot of people who speak Spanish were telling me like "You are Latina, you speak Spanish." Like a lot of, I hung out with a lot of American people then in high school then I felt like I was judged because I couldn't speak their Spanish and they say you act like a White girl now, but you are a Latin.
>
> Juan Ríos: Who called you that?
> Esperanza: Back in high school. Hispanic people told me that back in high school 'cause like every time they asked something in Spanish, I could not understand what they were saying but ah, ah, but then back in high school, and sophomore year I could understand some Spanish. I mean English, I made friends with some American girls.
> JR: Did you feel discriminated by other Latinos?
> Esperanza: Yeah, I felt discriminated by them. They said I pretended to be a White girl … instead of being my own self but it was different, I felt so different that not fitting within like them because I could not speak their language, a different language.
> JR: Did you feel more welcome with White people than with Latino people?
> Esperanza: Yeah, maybe because my foster family were American people and I didn't really have any Hispanic family here, so I felt like it was different. Yeah, and even in my previous school, I experienced being called "hey Mexican girl." I tell them, "Hey I am from Guatemala" and it is like well. It is so different.

It is important to highlight that Esperanza had a lot of challenges with social identities. First, when she arrived in the U.S., she only spoke a Mayan language from Guatemala, which made her feel isolated from the rest of Spanish-speaking Latinx students. Additionally, she was fostered by a White American woman. Although Esperanza's foster parent speaks Spanish, she can hardly communicate with her. Esperanza's internal conflicts were even worse when she tried to develop a cultural connection with other Latinx students since they (her peers) knew that she was living with a White family. Most of the time, her peers thought that she was not being honest about not being able to speak Spanish. Instead, they thought that she wanted to be Americanized. Urrieta (2003) states that:

> Issues of Latino identity are complex. The term is often used to include several other panethnic labels such as Hispanic, Chicano, or Mexican-American, often ignoring that Latinos inherit painful identity amalgamations from indigenous, European, and African worlds joined into a complex arrangement within Latin America and now Anglo-American society. (p. 149)

Esperanza's identity conflicts with both languages Spanish and English since most of her peers at home and church (her foster mother was an active member of a Christian church) were White and English speakers and so were her circle of friends. There were times when she dyed her hair and even started using blue contact lenses. It was like she wanted to detach herself from her Guatemalan/Latino culture to adopt a dominant White one.

Tracking and Low Expectations

A Difficult Class

The most difficult class that I have had was computer application 1 for many reasons. First, it was too difficult because I didn't speak English and I didn't understand what the teacher said. Second, I didn't type on the computer fast enough and when the teacher gave us some words to copy, I couldn't do it because I couldn't type fast. Third, sometimes the teacher asked us to read aloud and I couldn't read very well. Finally, it was difficult because I failed that class. (Santiago's journal)

One of the biggest challenges teenage Latinx immigrants experience in the U.S. schools is the English language. Because of their age, most of them are placed as freshmen in high schools. I remember a Mexican student who came to AHS as a freshman since he was already sixteen years old. Teachers started complaining about his lack of basic knowledge about the target language and math. When I talked to him about his prior education back in rural México, he shared with me that he never attended middle school back home (Suárez-Orozco & Suárez-Orozco, 2001). Unfortunately, this student did not find the necessary support to pursue his education. He ended up dropping out of school before his first semester was over.

Those students who become resilient, like Dulce, shared how they were held back since their high school courses taken back in their countries did not transfer to graduate in North Carolina. She shared,

> Me bajaron prácticamente cuatro años. En México me hacía falta un año para graduarme de la high school y aquí me pusieron en el grado 9, que viene siendo la secundaria que decimos en México. Que sería el tercero de secundaria. Me frustré.

I was lowered four years. In México, I needed one more year to graduate from high school and here I was placed in 9th grade, which is like middle school in México. It is like third grade in middle school. I got frustrated.

Dulce experienced a lot of frustration in the classroom since she acted more mature and focused than most teenage students. Before coming to the United States, she thought that she could graduate a year later; however, she discovered that she lacked the required courses more than the English language to graduate in the U.S. (Campos, 2013). There were some other instances when Latinx students were placed on less challenging courses assuming that because they were labeled ESL, they were not able to succeed in more advanced courses.

Besides the language challenge, Latinx students experience discrimination and racism based on stereotypes and prejudices against Spanish-speaking immigrants. Discrimination usually comes from unskilled teachers and counselors' low expectations while assigning courses for ESL and Latinx students. During the interviews, I asked the participants to reflect on their college preparedness courses when they were still in high school. I wanted to know if students were aware of the tracking system most students go through in this country. Gándara and Contreras (2009) posit that, "Clustering Latino students into the lower-level curriculum groups is a common practice in U.S. schools" (p. 97). Additionally, I wanted my students to become critically conscious about how prejudice and stereotyping toward ESL students and Latinx students impacted their academic success beyond high school. I asked Sofia if she felt she was placed in regular courses as a form of prejudice and she said,

Sí, sí lo siento porque yo pienso que conmigo lo hicieron en el aspecto de que no me querían ahí, a lo mejor poner en una clase donde ellos sabían que yo iba a fallarla por el idioma. Por miedo de que no la va pasar o no la va ser por eso hubiese preferido ponerme en unas clases básicas donde yo me mantuviera en un nivel básico

Yes, yes I feel it because they did it with me. I feel that they did not want to place me in a class where they knew I was not going to fail due to the language. They were afraid that I was not going to pass the class. For that reason, they placed me in basic courses.

Dulce added,

Juan Ríos: ¿Tú sabias que hay materias que se toman para ir a la universidad y otras que no?

Dulce: No, lo supé en el grado 10 u 11 porque usted me lo dijo de que tratara de tomar puras, bueno desde el principio usted me dijo que tratara de tomar puras clases avanzadas no las selectivas o clases sencillas nada más para agarrar los créditos.

Juan Ríos: Did you know that there are courses that will allow you to pursue higher education and others no?

Dulce: No, I knew about it in 10th and 11th grades because you told me to try to register to more advanced courses instead of regular courses to get more credits.

Once I realized that most of my students were placed in regular courses, I used my classroom to teach them how to navigate the tracking system. Having my K-12 education in Latin America and my knowledge about the Mexican educational system allowed me to better understand how different both educational systems were. Most of the time my students were not aware that they needed advanced courses to pursue higher education. I recall having unpleasant discussions with the school counselor about placing some of my students in low level courses due to the fact that they were identified as ESL. Valenzuela (1999) claims that, "ESL youth are regarded as limited English proficient rather than as Spanish dominant or potentially bilingual" (p. 173), assuming that their literacy skills in Spanish make them culturally and academically deficient; however, I knew that my students were capable of outperforming native English speakers. When I asked Francisco if he knew about advanced courses to pursue college, he shared:

F: Si, escuchaba que unas contaban más que las otras y unas que solo eran materias regulares. Tomé U.S. History. (prompted). Creo que sí tome un AP pero no recuerdo. Creo que sí era U.S. History. Sé que esas de AP te ayudaban para ir al colegio ... todo lo que era AP y Honors classes, pero solamente tome na' más algunas. Siento que mi caso fue más difícil como ya entre en el grado 9. Después como que tenías que tomar lo más difícil que era alcanzar hasta allá como los AP tenías que pasar los *Honors* y todo eso.

F: Yes, I used to hear that they counted more than others and that others were just regular courses. I took U.S. History. I think I took an AP course. I don't recall, I think it was U.S. History. I knew those AP helped me to go to college. All AP and Honor courses, but I only took a few. I feel that in my case, it was more difficult because I started in 9th grade. After like you had to take more difficult courses like to take AP courses, you had to pass honors and all of that.

JR: ¿Cuántas Honors tomaste?

Me: How many honors did you take?

F: Como tres o cuatro. Creo.

F: Like three or four. I think.

Francisco was a very committed student who loved to come to school. Many teachers liked him a lot. Although he worked very hard to get his high school diploma, he did not qualify for Deferred Action for Childhood Arrivals (DACA) since he arrived in this country after he turned sixteen (Bussert-Webb, Dizz, & Yanez, 2017). Later in the book I will talk about what happened to him after high school graduation.

Mauricio (an American citizen born and raised in Puerto Rico) and Santiago (a naturalized citizen born and raised in the Dominican Republic) decided to pursue higher education after high school; however, their experiences with racism and lack of support from faculty and a welcoming campus pushed them to change their minds about higher education (Gonzales, 2016). When I asked them how prepared they felt about college while still in high school, they responded.

Mauricio,

> **Juan Ríos:** Since you talked about freedom to choose your own courses in high school? Did somebody in school talk to you about the courses you need to take to pursue college?
> **Mauricio:** No, not that I remember.
> **JR:** Counselors, teachers. Did somebody tell you these courses do not make you college material?
> **Mauricio:** No that I remember.
> **JR:** Do you think you needed somebody who could talk to you about that?
> **Mauricio:** Yeah.
> **JR:** Did you realize that you were one of those non-college material students?
> **Mauricio:** No.
> **JR:** Do you know now?
> **Mauricio:** Oh yeah.

Mauricio's goal was to study auto-mechanic engineering; however, his reading and writing skills were very poor. During our conversations, he realized how hard it was for him to read long texts and to write academic essays. After paying his student loan, he decided to attend a private barber school. After he graduated from the barber school, he had a hard time getting his barber license. After a couple of trials, he finally got it. Last time I talked to him; he was working at a local barber shop in North Carolina. Similarly, Santiago's lack of knowledge about how to be prepared for college and his bad experience at a local community college led him to drop out.

Santiago,

> **Juan Ríos:** Did you know about college preparedness courses when you were in AHS?
> **Santiago:** I knew a little … not that much … I remember it was a counselor, but they only do it one time a year.
> **JR:** Did you take any of those courses?
> **Santiago:** I think I took some.
> **JR:** Did you take honors courses?
> **Santiago:** No never took them.
> **JR:** Did you take AP classes?
> **Santiago:** No never. They never told me to take those courses.
> **JR:** Do you think that AHS prepare you to go to college?

Santiago: Yo diría no mucho ... tal vez algunas clases si. Su clase pienso que si. Pero las otras no creo.

Santiago: I would say not that much. Maybe some classes. Your class, I think so. But the other ones, I don't think so.

JR:¿Cómo fue esa transición de alumno de high school a alumno de college?

JR: How was that transition from high school to college?

Santiago: En college no ayudan bastante. Los profesores no son iguales. No te dan la misma ayuda. Todo era diferente, las clases no me ayudaban tanto como en high school y se me hacía difícil también para las demás clases. Había que leer mucho y ese era uno de los problemas que había que leer mucho y mi inglés no era muy bueno.

Santiago: In college, they don't help you a lot. Professors are not the same. They don't give you the same support. It was all different. The classes. Nobody helped me like in high school. It was very difficult too in other courses. I had to read a lot and that was one of the problems that I had to read a lot and my English was not that good.

It is important to highlight that many students of color experience a lack of supportive system that can allow them to navigate higher education (Cammarota, 2008; Gándara & Contreras, 2009; Gonzales, 2016; Ríos Vega, 2015). When students of color attend predominantly White colleges, they experience a lot of stress for not being able to connect with individuals who can understand them, or they can see as positive role models. They either have to conform and internalize a colorblind and racist system or counteract racism and discrimination, which sometimes lead them to be seen as outcasts and culturally deficient (Conchas & Vigil, 2012; Rios, 2011, 2017).

As part of my research questions that led me to write this book, I asked my former students if their high school experience had prepared them to either get a good job or to pursue higher education. Again, Luz's and Sofia's answers showed a lack of knowledge about their high school education and how it prepared them or not to pursue higher education.

Luz,

Yo me sentí lista pero cuando uno mira la realidad no es así porque en todos los trabajos la high school viene siendo un certificado nada más, pero ellos van más afondo de tener más educación.

Luz: I felt ready, but when you like the reality, it is not that way because in all jobs a high school diploma is like another certificate, but they (employees) want you to have more education.

Sofia,

No, no lo creo, creo que la decisión de querer trabajar fue lo que empujó todo. Nunca recuerdo que me haigan dicho en la escuela algo de trabajo de por ejemplo tener un consejero designado que te diga en la escuela este es el camino, esto es lo que se hace. No, en la primera transición de mi escuela yo no sabía que clases me estaban dando, me estaban dando las que ellos querían, la que ellos pensaban me iban a ser bien a mi. Mi segundo año, tampoco me ayudó. Ahora yo me pongo a pensar en esos dos años. Yo siento de que yo perdió dos años en los que yo hubiese podido agarrar clases y enfocarme en lo que me iba ayudar a mí cuando saliera de la high school. *No, I don't think so. I think that my decision to wanting to get a job pushed everything. I don't recall that someone talked to me about job when I was in school. For example, having a counselor assigned that tells you in school how to do things. No, when I first transferred to high school, I did not know which classes they were giving me. They (counselors) gave me the ones they wanted; the ones they thought that were going to help me. During my second year, it did not help me either. Now that I think about those two years, I feel that I missed two years where I should have taken other courses and focused on courses that would help me after high school.*

It is clear that students like Sofia did not understand the tracking system in the U.S. I recall having serious conversations with Latinx parents and students about it during ESL parent's night or in the community. It is important to realize that many first-generation college students and immigrant families do not have the social capital and agency to help their children navigate a colorblind and racist school system. Most immigrant parents believe that sending their children to school will guarantee success and a better future; however, they are not aware of tracking system that sometimes keep their children trapped from going beyond k-12.

Juan Ríos: ¿Cuándo tú estabas estudiando en AHS tú sabias que habian materias que te preparan para la universidad y otras que no?

JR: When you were studying in AHS, did you know that some courses prepare you for college and others did not?

Sofia: No, yo no sabía eso. Me di cuenta después cuando mi hermano fue a la high school. Él empezó a decir que habían materias que podías tomar, hasta más avanzadas, materias que te podían ayudar a ahorrarte uno o dos años de colegio y luego que habían otros programas que te aceleraban mas tu récord académico en esas materias.

Sofia: No, I did not know that. I realized later when my brother went to high school. He started to say that there were courses that one could take, more advanced courses that could help you save one or two years of college and then that there were programs that could better your GPA while taking those courses.

JR: ¿Tu crees que a ti no te hablaron por el idioma?

JR: Do you feel that they did not talk to you about it because of the language?

Sofia: Si porque yo pienso que al saber que yo no hablaba inglés, porque en mi primer año me pusieron hacer unos exámenes GED y yo primer año yo recién llegada de El Salvador yo recuerdo que yo por mi apellido me acomodaron en un grupito de exámenes y yo todos los fallé. Yo nada mas circulaba. La maestra nada más me dijo con el lapicero que circulara pero que no lo podía tener blank, que tenía que circular el abc de esas respuestas. Mi segundo año ya en la high school yo sí pasé esos exámenes que me pusieron el año anterior.

Sofia: Yes because I feel that once they knew that I did not speak English because in my first year, they asked me to take the GED exam and I had recently arrived from El Salvador, I remember that because of my last name, they grouped me with a small group of students to take the test and I failed all of them. I only circled all of them. The teacher only told me that with the pencil I had to circle but that I could not leave it blank, that I had to circle the abc in the answers. My second year in high school, I passed the tests that they gave me the year before.

Like Sofia, many ESL newcomer students become victims of excessive testing and accountability. Most of the time they feel so scared and overwhelmed about all of this testing system that bombards ESL students. It is important to note that Sofia mentioned a GED test, which probes that she did not know which placement test she was given. Additionally, it is frustrating to realize how teachers encourage ESL newcomer students to complete those tests realizing that ESL newcomer students have no idea about the tracking system. Luz's comments about advanced courses to pursue higher education also show how little information ESL students actually understand about the educational system k-16 in the U.S.

Luz: Cuando las consejeras empezaron a hablar, pero ya era muy tarde para empezar a tomar esas materias. Me sentí triste, pero a la vez la podía tomar, pero las hubiése podido tomar en *high school*, que ahora me tocaba yo pagarlas en el college y un semestre tenía la opción, pagar el semestre o comprar los libros porque los libros también son bien costosos.

Luz: When the counselors started talking about it but it was too late to start taking those courses. I felt sad, but I had to take them. But if I had taken those courses while in high school, I did not have to pay for them. Now, I have to pay for them in college and one semester I had the option, to pay for the semester or to purchase the books, because the books are also very expensive.

Both Sofia and Luz benefited from DACA and decided to pursue higher education at a local community college. However, Luz could not continue due to health and family moral responsibilities. By the time I interviewed Sofia, she was taking one course online since her full-time job and motherhood obligations kept her busy.

Contrary, Elisa, Santiago's sister, became aware of her new challenges once she started attending the same community college. Throughout our conversations, I realized how hard Elisa had to work to challenge herself and social expectations. It was her courage and positive attitude that pushed her to learn how to navigate higher education.

> **Juan Ríos:** When did you realize that the courses you took at AHS did not prepare you to attend college?
>
> **Elisa:** It was the last semester because I was an early graduate so I didn't go from January to June, I believe or May. So I was out, so I was reading, I went to the RCC and I started like reading a lot of stuff and that's when I decided I wanted to transfer after graduation.
>
> **JR:** How did you fix that situation that some of your AHS courses did not help you?
>
> **Elisa:** (whispering and taking a deep breath). How can I explain it to you? I started researching by myself. I went online and learned things I couldn't learn in high school. Because first of all, I didn't know a lot of English. I mean of course you helped us a lot. But in my mind, having like a heavy accent, I felt like I didn't know a lot of English. I came at 16 and is harder than a child, but then I began researching about all that stuff about the community college and that's when I catch up. I know you helped us a lot in the ESL class, but I know I took a class in high school but I can't remember, which class it was but they used to change the teacher like they called them a lot in that semester, so basically I didn't learn a lot in that class. So I catch up by myself and the things that you taught us.
>
> **JR:** How did your high school experience prepare you to pursue higher education?
>
> **Elisa:** Not at all. I wasn't even thinking about RCC. Of course, we have counselors in high school, but they were leaning toward other students, like White and the Latinos we felt behind because I was talking to a lot of classmates like from México and other nationalities. The Latino community and we felt the same way, so they didn't prepare us well for that experience, so I had to find everything on myself.

Elisa learned first-hand how Latinx students felt discriminated at her high school. She realized how unprepared she felt after she finished high school (Gonzales, 2016; Ríos Vega, 2015). Instead, she understood that she needed to work harder than other students to remain in college and then transfer to a large institution to fulfill her dream of becoming a fashion designer. After the interview, Santiago and Elisa invited me to their house where her mother and father were waiting for us to have a delicious Dominican lunch. Afterwards, Elisa showed me her new fashion designs and talked to me about her first fashion designer contest participation.

Figure 1 As part of the International Club, my students and I did a lot of community service

Figure 2 We visited nursing homes, elementary schools and organized local events to showcase our Latinx heritages

Figure 3 Our International Club

Figure 4 The International Club represented a safe space for many ESL and minoritized students

Figure 5 Milagros and Karina on their graduation day

Figure 6 My student Victor and I after graduation

Figure 7 Students researched about Latin American countries and created carnival masks

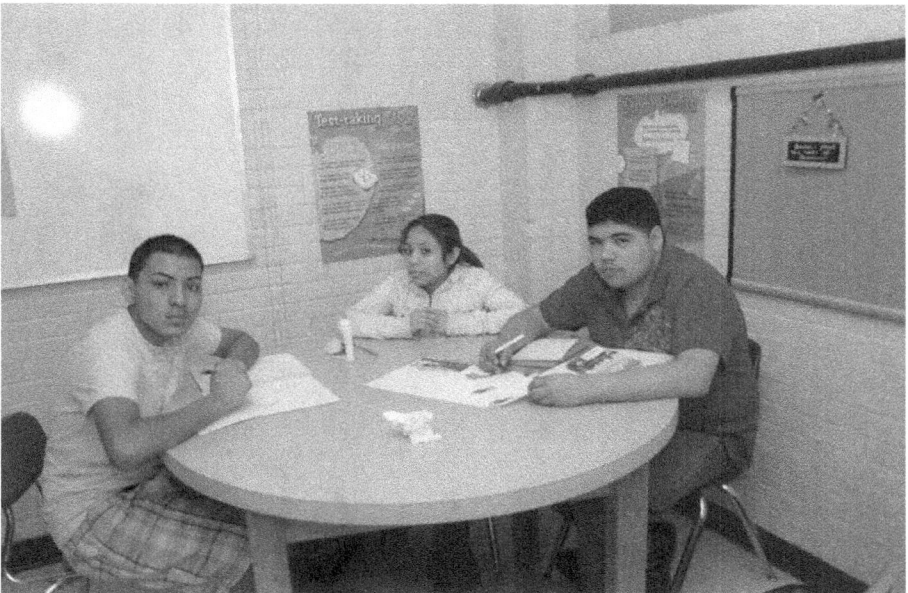

Figure 8 My students collaborating on their writing projects

Figure 9 The day my students published their journals

Figure 10 We decided to have a get together at the school library and to read some of their stories

Figure 11 Students published their book reports at the school library

Figure 12 In order to make them feel part of the school, I exhibited their works at the library

Undocuqueers

All I want
All I want is someone to help me
Someone who can teach me about life
Someone who can listen to me
All I want is someone to help me
Someone who can make me feel good
Someone to take me home
Someone to make me cry and laugh
All I want is someone to help me
Someone who can give me a hand
Someone to lead my way
Someone who can understand me
Someone who can feel proud of me
All I want is someone to share my life with
(Antonio's journal).

Teaching Latinx students and learning about their lives post-high school made me realize that some of them were also dealing with sexual identity challenges. As a teacher, I witnessed how some Latinx parents refused to accept their children's homosexuality. I recall seeing a couple from Costa Rica refusing to accept their daughter's girlfriend after reading some love letters. I also witnessed how other students of color were discriminated for being openly gay in school and how they were bullied and ignored at school events.

I will be referring to Dulce and Antonio as two Latinx undocuqueers as a political term used by undocumented queer and trans youth to name their gender, sexuality, and immigration status and to resist their feelings of fear and shame associated to their gender, sexuality, and immigration status (Cisneros & Bracho, 2019; Ríos Vega & Franeta, 2017).

It was through social media that I happened to know about Dulce's and Antonio's sexual orientation. When Dulce was my student, she used to attend her parents' Christian church and dated a Latino man. After high school, Dulce and I befriended on social media. I always noticed that Dulce made reference to another person but never unveiled her/his real gender until I asked her if that person was another woman and she said yes. During the interview, I also came out to Dulce as a queer man. Pérez (2012) states that, "Through relationships with teachers, undocumented students formed the trust necessary to disclose personal information about family circumstances and their immigrant status" (p. 37). I asked Dulce precise questions about her sexual orientation and her family's reaction to it.

JR: ¿Cuándo estabas en mi clase, tenias novio?

JR: When you were in my class, you had a boyfriend.

Dulce: Sí.

Dulce: Yes.

JR: ¿Cómo manejabas tu sexualidad en aquellos tiempos?

JR: How did you handle your sexuality during those times?

Dulce: Como mis papás siempre han sido cristianos, pues era como dice, "Para taparle el ojo al macho". Como para disimular las cosas, como para tratar de hacer las cosas bien conforme a ellos.

Dulce: Since my parents have always been Christians, well it was like the saying goes, "double standards." It was like to hide things, like trying to do the right things according to them.

JR: ¿Cuándo te das cuenta de que eres diferente a las demás chicas?

JR: When did you realize that you are different from other girls?

Dulce: Como desde los catorce o quince años que empecé a ver a las niñas diferente. Sentía como atracción. No era lo mismo con los varones. Con los varones solamente era salir a jugar y cosas así. Por eso casi nunca me llevaba con las mujeres porque siempre era me van a ver, se van a dar cuenta o voy a sentir raro. Cosas así. Me juntaba más con los varones. Primera, a las mujeres les gusta más el drama y es algo que no me gusta. A mi siempre me gustaba lo que era fútbol, andar corriendo y hacer cosas que a las demás no les gustaba.

Dulce: Like when I was fourteen or fifteen when I started seeing girls differently. I felt an attraction toward them. It was not the same with the boys. With the boys, I used to play and things like that. For that reason, I almost never got along with girls because I always wondered if they would realize or notice or maybe I wanted to avoid feeling weird. Things like that. I used to hang out with boys. First, women love drama and it is something that I don't like. I always loved soccer, running, and to do things that girls didn't like.

JR: ¿Tu familia sabe que eres lesbiana?

JR: Does your family know you are lesbian?

Dulce: Lo sabe pero es un tema que nunca se ha tocado. Lo saben porque se han dado cuenta por mis parejas, por las personas con las que he vivido. Pero abiertamente a que yo les diga, no. Es un tema que no me atrevo a tocar con ellos. Será por no defraudarlos porque no es lo que ellos quieren para mi. Bueno mi mamá siempre me ha querido tocar el tema, pero yo siempre le doy la vuelta. Incluso mi papá un año me dijo, "Te prefiero puta que lesbiana." Porque se daban cuenta de cómo soy y a ellos eso les eno-jaba. Nunca me lo dijeron abiertamente, pero siempre hacian comentarios. Me sentía mal porque siempre he querido el apoyo de ellos en cuanto a esa forma y es algo que yo simplemente sé que no va a pasar. Mis hermanos si saben. Se los he dicho y conocen y conviven con mi pareja. Mi pareja tiene 41.

Han sido tres antes de esta. Todas ha sido en los Estados Unidos. Nunca me atreví a tener pareja en México. México siempre es el que dirán, las críticas, es más fuerte todo.

Dulce: They know about it, but it is a topic that we have never talked about. They know because they have seen my partners, for the people that I have lived with. I have never told them openly. It is a topic that I don't dare to talk to them about. I will feel like I am betraying them because it is not what they want for me. Well, my Mom has always wanted to talk to me about the topic, but I always try to avoid it. As a matter of fact, my Dad said one year, "I prefer my daughter to be prostitute than a lesbian." Because they noticed the way I am and that made them feel mad. They never told me this openly, but they always made comments. I felt bad because I have always wanted their support toward my sexuality and it's something that I know will never happen. My siblings know about it. I have told them and have seen and talked to my partner. My partner is 41.

JR: ¿Has sufrido opresión por ser lesbiana?

JR: Have you suffered for being lesbian?

Dulce: Solo una vez en Texas cuando tenía una pareja. Viví un año en Tejas. La gente se espantaba y empezaban a decir cosas como porque iban de la mano. "Cochinas", y siempre había insultos de Latinos. En Carolina del Norte no he sufrido opresión social de la gente. He sufrido más opresión social por ser Latina.

Dulce: Only once in Texas when I used to have a partner. I lived in Texas for one year. People used to be in shock and started to say things because we were holding hands, "Nasty," and there were always slurs coming from Latinos. In North Carolina, I have not suffered oppression from people. I have experienced more oppression for being Latina.

Dulce's comments about her sexual orientation are not uncommon in most Latinx families. Although her parents know about her sexuality, they prefer to avoid talking about it as it did not exist while other family members make homophobic comments to avoid talking about the topic although they are aware of their children's sexuality. It is important to highlight how Dulce did not want to show her sexual attraction for girls when she was living with her relatives in México due to her age or to avoid being disowned. It was not until she finished high school and moved away from her parents in the U.S. when she decided to move in with her first female partner in Texas. Misa (2001) argues that Chicana/o queers prefer to hide their queer identity to get emotional and social support from their own kin, leading them to experience internal conflicts and tensions.

Like Dulce, Antonio's narratives about his homosexuality were not shared until after he completed high school and became independent from his mother and two brothers. Interestingly, at the beginning of the interview, Antonio identified himself as bisexual; however, as he became more relaxed, he changed it to being gay. During the interview, I noticed that Antonio avoided talking about being harassed or discriminated for being openly gay at school. Instead he shared how much he ignored homophobic comments from his peers, especially his own community. He said,

Honestamente, no. Yo creo que no importa tu preferencia sexual. Como yo lo he tomado es quién eres. Porque mis compañeros hacían comentarios así, pero yo nunca lo tomé como algo homofóbico como una burla hacia mí porque yo creo que yo siempre me he definido como soy. Por eso no me pongo una etiqueta. Es que yo sé quien soy y no tengo que aclararle al mundo quién soy porque al final las personas siempre van a tener otra vista de ti. Entonces a mi nunca me importó lo que dijeran, o si lo decian jugando, o si lo decían en serio porque al final del día yo sabía quién era.

Honestly, no. I don't think your sexual preference matters. I have taken it as who you are. Because my classmates made comments like that, but I never took them as homophobic, like bullying toward me because I think that what have defined me is to be who I am. For that reason, I don't label myself. I know who I am, and I don't have to explain the world who I am because at the end, people will always see you the other way. Then I never cared what people said or if they said while joking or if they were serious about their comments because at the end of the day, I knew who I was.

JR: ¿Pero sí pasó?

JR: But did it happen?

Antonio: Si, pasó. Simplemente yo no lo tomé así. Tal vez si era ofensivo o realmente se referían a eso pero no lo tomé así. Los comentarios venían de mis propios compañeros Hispanos.

Antonio: Yes, it happened. I didn't take it that way. Maybe it was offensive o they really meant it but I didn't take that way. The comments came from my Hispanic classmates.

JR: ¿Tienes pareja?

JR: Do you have a partner right now?

Antonio: No, pero si he tenido. He tenido dos parejas. Tengo 25 años.

Antonio: No, but I have had. I have had two partners. I am 25 years old.

JR: ¿Cuándo te diste cuenta de que eras diferente?

JR: When did you realize that you were different?

Antonio: Fue a la edad de 18 años. Cuando después de una fiesta un hombre me besó. Fue cuando me hizo pensar diferente.

Antonio: It was when I was 18 years old. When the party was over, a man kissed me. It made me think differently.

It is clear that Antonio always understood his homosexuality. Whether he was consciously aware or not about being bullied or not by his own peers, he realized that due to his sexuality he had no choice but to internalize homophobia as a norm (Ríos Vega & Franeta, 2017).

I also asked Antonio about his mother's reaction about his sexuality. Like Dulce, Antonio agreed by saying that his mother knew about him being gay, but she refused to talk about it. Instead, she used religion to make him change his sexuality. He said,

Ella sabe (his Mom). Típico de una familia hispana. Siempre el rechazo. Querer cambiarte y lavarte el cerebro para hacerte cambiar, pero tú sabes lo que eres. Pero como yo digo yo creo que depende de cada persona que no esté segura de lo que es y que tenga que enfrentar lo que es.

She knows (his Mom). It is common in a Hispanic family. There is always rejection. They want to change you and brainwash you to make you change, but you already know who you are. But like I say, I think it depends on each person that is not sure about who he/she is and has to face it.

JR: ¿Qué cosas te dice para lavarte el cerebro?

JR: What things were you told to brainwash you?

Antonio: Como busca de Dios, ir a la iglesia para cambiar. Pero obviamente sabemos que no va a pasar. Ha habido cierta fricción en la familia por esto. Mi hermano (Francisco) simplemente dijo que esa era mi decisión que él no tenía nada que comentar.

Antonio: Find God, go to church, so you can change. But obviously, we know that it is not going to happen. There has been some friction in my family because of it. My brother (Francisco) simply said that it was my decision that he didn't have any comments to make about it.

It is very common to see how Latinx families use their religious beliefs to make their children change their sexual orientation (Kumashiro, 2001). However, like Antonio stated some Hispanic families tend to reject and disown their children. In this case, Dulce and Antonio preferred to move away from their parents, to either live with their partner like Dulce or to live their sexuality in less hostile environment. In the next section, I document the narratives of the participants who decided to start their own families and who had no choice but to get jobs instead of pursuing higher education.

ESL Class

That Teacher

That teacher is my favorite one for many reasons. First, he tries to help everyone especially Hispanics. He is my favorite because I have learned a lot with him. Second, I have learned English with him. Also, he makes us reflect about life with his sermons. Third, he helps us to be responsible and fight for our goals. He always tells us to study hard to be someone in life, but most of us don't care of what he says. Finally, he is my favorite teacher because he helps us learn English, and not to be in trouble. His name is Mr. Ríos. (Santiago's journal)

I quit my teaching job at AHS in 2012 to pursue my dream of becoming a university faculty and to echo my Latinx students' experiences in education in the U.S. One of the many reasons why I decided to write this book was to document how students' journeys in our schools shape their lives during and after they get their high school diploma. Although it was not my intention to document how I impacted my students' lives, while interviewing my former students, I learned how my words and actions made them feel. It was to my surprise to realize that some students came to school because of me. Some asked their parents to pay an extra fee to stay at AHS because of my sense of care and love to advocate for their education and empathy while teaching. Hooks (1994) states that, "When teachers work to affirm the emotional well-being of students, we are doing the work of love" (p. 133). Other students carried out my words of wisdom to pursue higher education and decided to move back to their homelands. Like me, other teachers also did their part. Those who became their students' role models, friends, and confidants are recalled in this section of this book.

When I was teaching, I always felt excited to see my students coming to class every day since many of them, especially boys, got in trouble at school or the community due to gang activities or by breaking the law. Some of them got caught by the police while driving without a license since most of them were undocumented. In addition, some girls also became pregnant or ran away with their boyfriends. Every time I heard someone had dropped out of school, my heart broke into pieces. I wanted all of my students to succeed in school. I guessed my students understood my message since I used to give them regular lectures about the importance of staying in school and to graduate. Freire (1998) said, "My openness to caring for the well-being of my students has to do with my openness to life itself, to the joy of living" (p. 125). After knowing about my students' personal journeys before and while coming to the U.S., I learned to see them as my heroes. Most of them were already 16 years and by law no one could change their minds about dropping out of school if they wanted to do it. In other words, seeing my students at school every day gave me hope to continue doing my work as a teacher and role model.

During the interview, I wanted to find out what made them stay in school and graduate. I wanted to know about their favorite class.

> Elisa: …(thinking). Being in your class (laughing) definitely. It wasn't the same. By then, I was taking PE and history, and being involved in like in the Latino … in like the ESL class like a lot of Latino students, so I felt more confident and it was helpful. You used to help me a lot.
> Santiago: I think your class was my favorite thing because I learned a lot. You helped me a lot. That's one of the good things.
> JR: Do you remember that day when you were crying in school?
> Santiago: Yeah. I cried because I didn't understand any class. They were talking in English and I didn't know what they were saying, and I felt frustrated. (We recalled the whole incident when a teacher brought him down to my room for, he was crying, and she didn't know what to do.)
> JR: I was glad I was there.
> Santiago: (laughing). Me too.

> Gloria: En la época de high school … yo creo que diría directamente ESL porque me sentía más en familia … éramos de diferentes culturas, asiáticos, latinos, etc.

> *Gloria: During high school, I would say ESL because I felt like a family. We came from different cultures, Asians, Latinos, etc.*

> Diana: Honestamente sí era mi clase de ESL porque me gustaba eso, se me hacía mas fácil para aprender. Cómo que lo tenía más claro que en las otras clases. En las otras clases eran, por ejemplo eran requisito para graduarme y la verdad no le puse mucha importancia porque como no era algo de mi país, algo histórico, historias de mi país, tal vez alguna clase que so no le puse mucha importancia.

> *Diana: Honestly, my ESL class because I liked it. I found it easy to learn. Like I understood it better than other classes. The other classes were, for example, a requisite to graduate, and to be honest I did not pay so much attention because it was not something from my country, something historical from my country, maybe a class that I did not care.*

> Antonio: Me acuerdo la convivencia con los demás compañeros. Y qué era una de las clases donde nos podíamos abrir un poquito más, no tanto como estudiantes sino como personalmente. Interactuar con diferentes culturas y también porque allí siempre teníamos ayuda de las otras clases que teníamos. También nos involucrabamos más con la comunidad en ayudar y aprendíamos cosas más diferentes que lo de una escuela regular.

Antonio: *I recall the coexistence with other classmates. And it was a class where we could open up a little bit more, not only as students but personally. We used to interact with different cultures and also there we also had support for other classes we had. Also, we got involved with the community to help and to learn different things more than a regular school.*

Sofia: Mi última clase cuando llegué, que miré el letrero del número de la clase que me tocaba. Cuando conocí a Mr. Ríos, me sentí como más aliviada porque todos los que estaban en la clase pues eran hispanos y hablaban español. El maestro hablaba español pues eso me hacía sentir mejor, el estar en la escuela con esa clase porque yo sentía de que alguien me entendía, que alguien sabía lo que yo decía, que hablamos el mismo idioma, que posiblemente hasta nos gustaba la misma comida. Él Fue algo mejor. ESL fue algo que hizo que la escuela no fuera tan estresante porque tener todas las clases en las que yo no entendía nada al llegar a una donde yo podía finalmente hablar fue un alivio.

My last class when I came that I saw the sign and the number that I had class. When I met Mr. Ríos, I felt like more released because all of the students in that class were Hispanic and spoke Spanish. The teacher spoke Spanish. That made me feel better. To be in school in that class I felt that somebody understood me, that somebody knew what I was saying, and that we spoke the same language, that maybe we even liked the same food. It was so much better. ESL made the school less stressful because having all of those classes where I did not understand anything and come to a class where I could finally talk was a relief.

Luz: A mí lo que me gustaba de high school. Honestamente me gustaba más estar en ESL porque allí aparte de una clase era como una familia. Estar con otros estudiantes de nuestra misma cultura, las mismas raíces. Teníamos como la misma historia. Nos relacionábamos con la misma historia, de las dificultades que uno pasa recién llega y a los pasos que íbamos. Pero siempre estuvo Mr. Ríos que siempre nos dio como un apoyo. Él siempre nos daba motivo para seguir adelante y para seguir aprendiendo.

Luz: What I liked the most in high school. Honestly, I liked to be in ESL because there besides being a class, it was like a family. To be with other students from the same culture, the same roots. We had like the same stories. Our stories were related to each other, the difficulties that we went through when we arrived and the steps that we were taking. But Mr. Ríos was always there, giving us support. He always gave us a reason to move ahead and to continue learning.

Julio: My second semester, I started attending your ESL class and I liked your class 'cause I felt it was a place, a classroom where you could be you. And you didn't have anybody that would start laughing at the way you spoke English, the way you dress, the way you look, the way you express yourself, 'cause everybody in your class, we were all Latino, remember. So, I liked your class a lot too because I felt like I was accepted. You can say, in your classroom, where I didn't have these conflicts.

Diana: La clase de ESL se me hacía mas interesante porque en esa clase era donde yo tenía la oportunidad de expresarme, de expresar mi naturaleza, no tenía que esforzarme tal vez para ser como los otros compañeros. So era el lugar donde yo me sentía yo misma. Era el lugar donde yo me sentía mas cómoda.

Diana: Yes, it was more interesting because in that class I had the opportunity to express myself, my nature. I did not have to make an effort to be myself. It was a place where I felt myself. It was the place where I felt comfortable.

Using the ESL classroom as a nurturing space was the greatest opportunity as a Latinx teacher. hooks (1994) argues that, "When as teachers we teach with love, combining care, commitment, knowledge, responsibility, respect, and trust, we are often able to enter the classroom and go straight to the heart of the matter" (p. 134). My classroom, which used to be a photography classroom in the basement, became like a sacred haven for me and my students. We felt free to talk about personal, familial, and social issues without fear of being looked down or punished. It was also a healing space for me since I realized that my students and I shared many things in common. My students and I had the same stories with racism, gender and language discrimination, and racial profiling as immigrants to the U.S. I reminded them that in the school I had some type of privilege as a teacher; however, out in the community I experienced the same type of discrimination and oppression that most Latinx immigrants face daily.

To support a culturally sensitive pedagogy and curriculum, I exposed my students to different Latinx writers such as Sandra Cisneros, Gary Soto, Isabel Allende, Pat Mora, and many others, my students and I discussed and unpacked a lot of issues that were closely related to our lives as immigrants to the U.S. I used my role as a teacher to give "consejos" (advice) (Villenas & Deyhle, 1999) to my students about life, education, and their futures. Some of my students shared with me how much they disliked reading before taking my class.

Juan Ríos: ¿Qué recuerdas que yo decía?

Juan Ríos: Do you remember what I used to say?

Luz: je, je, je, specialmente algo que aprendí fue encontrarle amor a la lectura, como yo nunca, nunca lo había hecho. No le veía el significado de leer un libro. Eso se me hacia aburrido, algo así, pero cuando usted no enseñó así como a saborear un libro, a ver el mensaje que tenía un libro. Eso sí me ayudó mucho y me abrió mucho mis pensamientos.

Luz: He, he, he. Specially, something I learned was to find love for reading. Like I've never, never done it. I did not see any purpose to read a book. It was boring, something like that. It helped me a lot. And opened my mind, my thoughts.

Juan Ríos: Do you remember something you learned in that class?

Elisa: Oh my God, it has been so long … Definitely, what I learned was that I needed to be someone because of what I heard about other students like dropping out of school or they couldn't go to other university due to their legal status. So, I wanted to be someone different.

One of the biggest surprises during the interviewing process was to hear Gloria's comments about her education after high school and how my words impacted her life. hooks (2003) states,

> When teachers and students evaluate our learning experiences, identifying the classes that really matter to us, no one gives testimony about how much they learned from professors who were disassociated, unable to connect, and self-obsessed (p. 129).

As her former ESL teacher, I never knew that my *consejo* (advice) was taken so seriously until she mentioned it to me.

Juan Ríos: ¿Cuál fue el motivo que te hizo regresar a México a seguir estudiando?

Juan Ríos: What was the reason why you decided to go back to México to continue your studies?

Gloria: cuando estaba directamente en el 11 que tenía prácticamente unos 16 años estaba en la clase ESL, vamos directamente hablando de nuestro futuro, vamos a llegar a la etapa de senior. Mr. Ríos fue el que me motivó a que siguiera estudiando. Me ayudó completamente a que yo buscara una universidad. Él fue el que animó, podemos decir que fue mi role model, mi modelo a seguir. Él me contó su historia. Él fue el que me dijo, *"ve a México y lucha por lo que quieres".*

Gloria: When I was in 11th grade that I was 16 years, I was in the ESL class and we were talking about our futures and when we reach senior. Mr. Ríos was who motivated me to continue my education. He helped me to find a university. He encouraged me. I can say that he was my role model. He told me his story. He told me, "Go to México and fight for what you want."

I recall when Gloria called me on her way back to México. She shared that a private university had accepted her. Honestly, I wanted to see her and wish her the best of luck, but I was living in a different town when she called me. When I interviewed Gloria, she was visiting her parents back in North Carolina. She graduated from college and was currently working for a hotel chain in Cancún, México.

The most effective teacher

The most effective teacher that I have had is Mr. Ríos. You have always been there to advise me about life and its dangers. You are one of the fewest teachers that had gained my confidence with. Also, you are the one who completely convinced me to go to college and become somebody. Before I met you, I was just going to finish high school and go straight to work. Thanks to your "regaños" and advice, I realized how important it is to get an education and have a profession. Due to that is why now I put all my effort into my studies, and I have all that desire to go to college. I'm really thankful for everything you have done for me. I have never had a teacher like you that cares about me, my education and my future. (Mauricio's journal)

Mauricio's journal entry really touched me since he was one of my very last students before getting a faculty job in the Midwest. He is the only student that I still advise and mentor. Although his dreams to pursue higher education changed after he realized it was too hard for him, I still advised him to study something that he felt passionate about. hooks (2003) claims that "All meaningful love relations empower each person engaged in the mutual practice partnership. Between teacher and student love makes recognition possible" (p. 136). Every time I go back to North Carolina, I find the time to meet Mauricio and to check up what is going on in his life.

My Best Teacher

First, I want to thank God for all my teachers because they are wonderful and great. One of them is Mr. Ríos, Juan because he is like a father at school and he gave us a lot of advice. Also, he teaches us a lot of things from life and how important is our culture and also, we had to be proud of our countries. He is a special person in my life because he gives me a lot of advice, and he is always telling me that I have to do good things.

Also, I admire him because he always is helping the community and all those people who need his help. Also, his demonstrates to other people that we are Latinos and not all of them are bad. No because a couple of them are bad that means that not everyone is the same. Also, I have learned from him what is respect to other people, and it is necessary that we show others that we can do something for this country using our cultures, and never forget where we are from. Also, he is always telling us that we have to graduate to have a better life and job.

No matter where we are, no matter where you go but with your degree, we could do anything we want or with an education we can be independent no matter the obstacle. Finally, I respect him because he respects me, and he is like my second father at school even when he is just my ESL teacher. Also, if he is watching me doing something bad, he is always telling me that I have to stop doing that. No matter where I am, I will respect him because I have learned a lot from him.

I hope that every day I can learn more things from him. He will always be in a special place in my heart. God bless him. (Katie's journal)

I decided to close this chapter with Katie's journal entry. I never met a student who had been through so much in life like Katie. When I met and learned about Katie's journey to this country, she became my role model and hero. She was always optimistic about life and school. She always volunteered to organize choreographies around Hispanic Heritage Month, Mother's Day, community service at nursing homes, and Día de la Raza (Hispanic Festival). She also taught her peers how to dance *punta*, a traditional Garifuna dance of Honduras. As you have read, my students were more than names and students, they were my *familia*. They gave me hope to be a better human being. Most of them are already parents while others are working and studying. A lot of them are my friends on social media so I can still be in touch with them and their new families and friends.

Summary

This chapter analyzed how the participants' experiences with discrimination shaped their lives and well-being while they were in high school. Some of them shared how their teachers discriminated against them for speaking in Spanish in the classroom. Instead of seeing their native language as part of their linguistic capital and classroom asset, they were seen as a barrier to assimilate the dominant (White) culture. Additionally, other students' classification as ESL made them victims of low expectations, pushing them to get trapped in a tracking system. Most of these students were placed in regular and racially segregated classrooms. It was very common to witness students of color (usually African American and Latinx) internalize this form of colorblindness and discrimination as the norm. Finally, this chapter discusses how the participants made strong connections with me. I also documented how Dulce's and Antonio's experiences with issues of race/ethnicity, immigration status, and class intersect their sexual orientation, which I refer to them as undocuqueers. It is important to understand that individuals like Dulce and Antonio face double marginalization and oppression than other Latinx students.

Like I mentioned earlier in this chapter, it was not my intention to document how my love sense of love, care, and passion for teaching impacted my students' lives. I was very impressed to hear how my former students recalled my words and actions to support and to advocate for them. The next chapter will analyze what happened to the participants after they obtained their high school diploma.

References

Arriaza, G. (2004). Welcome to the front seat: Racial identity and Mesoamerican immigrants. *Journal of Latinos and Education*, 3(4), 251–265.

Bussert-Webb, K., Díaz, M. E., & Yanez, K. A. (2017). *Justice & space matter in a strong, unified Latino community*. New York, NY: Peter Lang Publishing, Inc.

Cammarota, J. (2008). *Sueños Americanos: Barrio youth negotiating social and cultural identities*. California: The University of Arizona Press.

Campos, D. (2013). *Educating Latino boys: An asset-based approach*. Thousand Oaks, CA: Corwin.

Cisneros, J., & Bracho, C. (2019). Coming out of the shadows and the closet: Visibility schemas among undocuqueer immigrants. *Journal of homosexuality, 66*(6), 715–734.

Conchas, G. Q., & Vigil, J. D. (2012). *Streetsmart schoolsmart: Urban poverty and the education of adolescent boys*. New York, NY: Teachers College Press.

Freire, P. (1998). *Pedagogy of freedom: Ethics, democracy, and civic courage*. Lanham, MD: Rowman & Littlefield Publishers, Inc.

Gándara, P. C., & Contreras, F. (2009). *The Latino education crisis: The consequences of failed social policies*. Cambridge, MA: Harvard University Press.

Gay, G. (2010). *Culturally responsive teaching: Theory, research, and practice* (2nd ed.). New York, NY: Teachers College.

Gonzales, R. G. (2016). *Lives in limbo: Undocumented and coming of age in America*. Oakland: University of California Press.

Hooks, B. (1994). *Teaching to transgress: Education as the practice of freedom*. New York: Routledge.

Hooks, B. (2003). *Teaching community: A pedagogy of hope*. New York, NY: Routledge.

Kozol, J. (2012). *Savage inequalities: children in Americas schools*. New York: Broadway Paperbacks.

Kumashiro, K. K. (2001). *Troubling intersections of race and sexuality: Queer students of color and anti-oppressive education*. Boston Way, Lanham, MD: Rowman & Littlefield Publishers, Inc.

Menjívar, C. (2002). Living in two worlds? Guatemalan-origin children in the United States and emerging transnationalism. *Journal of Ethnic and Migration Studies, 28*(3), 531–552.

Misa, C. M. (2001). Where have all the queer students of color gone? Negotiated identity of queer Chicana/a students. In K. K. Kumashiro (Ed.), *Troubling intersections of race and sexuality: Queer students of color and anti-oppressive education* (pp. 67–80). New York, NY: Rowman and Littlefield Publishers, Inc.

Pérez, W. (2012). *Americans by heart: Undocumented Latino students and the promise of higher education*. New York, NY: Teachers College Press.

Rios, V. M. (2011). *Punished: Policing the lives of Black and Latino boys*. New York, NY: NYU Press.

Rios, V. M. (2017). *Human targets: Schools, police, and the criminalization of Latino youth*. Chicago, IL: The University of Chicago Press.

Ríos Vega, J. (2015). *Counterstorytelling narratives of Latino teenage boys: From Verguenza to Echale Ganas*. New York, NY: Peter Lang Publishing.

Ríos Vega, J., & Franeta, S. (2017). DREAMers in double exile: Teachers can be allies to LGBTQ students. In S. Wong, S. Sanchez Gosnell, A. M. Foerster Luu, & L. Dodson (Eds.), *Teachers as allies: Transformative practices for teaching DREAMers and undocumented students* (pp. 108–120). New York, NY: Teachers College Press.

Suárez-Orozco, C., & Suárez-Orozco, M. M. (2001). *Children of immigration*. Boston, MA: Harvard University Press.

Urrieta, L. (2003). Las identidades también lloran, identities also cry: Exploring the human side of indigenous Latina/o identities. *Educational Studies, 34*(2), 147–212.

Valenzuela, A. (1999). *Subtractive schooling: US-Mexican youth and the politics of caring.* Albany, NY: Sunny Press.

Villenas, A. M., & Lucas, T. (2002). *Educating culturally responsive teachers: A coherent approach.* Albany, NY: State University of New York Press.

Villenas, S., & Deyhle, D. (1999). Critical race theory and ethnographies challenging the stereotypes: Latino families, schooling, resilience and resistance. *Curriculum Inquiry, 29*(4), 414–445.

Yosso, T. J., Smith, W. A., Ceja, M., & Solórzano, D. G. (2009). Critical race theory, racial microaggressions, and campus racial climate for Latina/o undergraduates. *Harvard Educational Review, 79*(4), 659–690.

CHAPTER FOUR

Post-High School

My Goals in Life

I have many goals in my life, but the first one is to finish high school to go to college because I want to be an engineer or an architect. I want to go to college not because my family wants me to go, but because I want to go to college. I want to go to college because I want to have a better future for me and my family. Finally, I want to be a baseball player because that's my favorite sport. (Santiago's journal)

Introduction

When Santiago wrote his journal entry, his goals of attending college and becoming a professional were very clear since he wanted to please his parents. Also, like many Dominican boys, he wanted to become a professional baseball player. However, all of his aspirations and dreams get broken once he started attending a local community college where he experienced invisibility and racism from his professors. These bad experiences led him to drop out and start working at a local auto parts store.

Reconnecting with some of my former students after 10 years allowed us to bring back memories about their school experiences and challenges. During our interviews, we caught up about families, friends, and new families. It was also painful for me as I chose to hold the interviews at a local library, which I used to visit when I first moved to North Carolina. However, I was eager to hear what had happened in my former students' lives after they had finished high school. I knew some of them did not pursue higher education due to their immigration status or family responsibilities; however, I wanted to learn how my former students became resilient and found hope post-high school education. In this chapter, I analyze what happened to my former students who wanted to attend college and could not due to their immigration status and arrival to the U.S. I discuss how some of them benefitted from Deferred Action for Childhood Arrivals (DACA) while others did not. Additionally, I document how Sofia, Esperanza, and Elisa learned to navigate college and how some others, like Santiago, Mauricio, and Luz ended up dropping out. Also, I analyze how Gloria and Julio decided to move back to México and graduated from college. Finally, I document how Dulce's and Antonio's experiences as undocuqueers, and coming out after high school shape their relationship with their parents and relatives. I close this chapter talking about Diana's, Sofia's, and Luz's new families and family moral responsibilities.

College and DACA

Mauricio, Esperanza, Elisa, Santiago, Sofia, and Luz decided to pursue higher education in the U.S. while Gloria and Julio moved back to México to accomplish their college dreams. Unfortunately, Mauricio, Santiago, and Luz ended up dropping out due to lack of mentorship and financial support. Pérez (2012) states that adults can serve Latinx students as role models to set high expectations, build confidence by believing in their academic skills, and encourage them to pursue college. By the time I did my interviews, Esperanza and Sofia were still attending college. Esperanza, who was a full-time student, had transferred to a private university after spending three years at a local community college. She shared with me how hard college was for her and how many times she had to either drop off course and/or change majors. Sofia was taking online courses at a local community college. She had to split her time as a single mother, full-time fast-food restaurant manager, and part-time student. Francisco, Diana, Antonio, and Dulce decided not to pursue higher education due to their lack of information about college, their immigration status in this country, and family moral responsibilities (Gonzales, 2016; Valdés, 1996).

At the beginning of this chapter, I started with Santiago's journal entry about his goals in life. Like I mentioned, although he finished high school with big dreams about becoming a professional, his frustrations while at a local community college pushed him to abandon his dreams. After he finished high school, he worked at a fast-food restaurant for one year after he decided to attend a local community college. When I asked him why he left college, he talked about being the only Latino in class and feeling invisible in the classroom. He said,

> Los profesores se inclinaban más en los americanos que en ayudarme a mi (*professors preferred to support Americans instead of helping me*). Y me cansé (*and I got tired of it*), so I left. I think it was 2012, so maybe six years or five years. I was taking graphic design. I completed one year.

Hurtado, Haney, and Hurtado (2012) argue that, "There are few spaces where young men of Color can explore becoming full human beings, possessing all of the vulnerabilities, hope, love, trust, and openness that the journey entails" (p. 115). By the time, I interviewed Santiago, he was working at a car parts store, fixing dent vehicles. He was not happy with his salary. He thought about starting a home business with his father. I also learned that Santiago was getting through a divorce after he married a Dominican woman. He shared,

> I'm married. I mean separated. I got married when I was 23 for three or four years. I don't remember. Now I'm going through a divorce. No children. We were not getting along, so and I think I was too young to get married. She's Dominican. She lives in New York.

Like Santiago's experience in college, Mauricio also decided to drop out of college after his freshman year. He said,

> I was happy. I was glad I got out of school because I didn't like school. I just find out they teach you stuff that makes no sense. That probably won't help you in your future, like science.

When I asked him if he felt high school prepared him for college, his response was

> No. because when I first thought about what I wanted to study; high school didn't teach me automobile technician. So high school doesn't teach you anything about electricity, cars unless you choose to take it. And not always they have those classes for you to take. And now that I want to learn how to be a barber, they don't teach you those things in high school. It didn't really help me.

> Pues cuando estaba estudiando pensaba que mecánico era lo que me iba a gustar. Estaba cogiendo auto body y me gustaba. Pero cuando de verdad empecé a conocer lo que era, no me gustó. Tiene muchas cosas que no me gustan, como la electricidad. Si. Todos los carros ahora son eléctricos. Nunca me ha gustado lidiar con cables y había que leer mucho.

> *Well, when I was studying, I thought I wanted to be an auto mechanic. I was taking auto body and I liked it. But when I really started to know what it was, I did not like it. It has*

many things that I do not like, like electricity. Yes. All cars now are electric. I have never liked
the idea of dealing with cables and I had to read a lot.

Both Santiago and Mauricio tried to pursue higher education; however, a lack of a supportive system and mentorship even before attending college, pushed them to change their minds about their dreams. Santiago shared how feeling invisible in the classroom made him experience racism and discrimination for being Latino. He missed the fact that the nurturing and caring environment that he experienced in high school was not present in college. Also, the fact that he did not see faculty members who he could connect or relate with made him wonder about pursuing a college degree (Conchas & Vigil, 2012; Irizarry, 2011). Likewise, Mauricio's narratives talk about how ill-prepared he felt after finishing high school and lack of knowledge about what he thought he wanted to pursue in college. It is clear that high school counselors or teachers did not talk to him about college life and how demanding it might be. While I was his teacher, I noticed that Mauricio was a very introverted student, who hardly talked to mainstream students. However, I learned more about him and his goals through his writings.

My Future Life

In the future, I will graduate from college and will have a profession in automotive repair. I would have my own shop. I will get married and have my own family. I'm going to be probably married with Nancy (fake name). I plan to have two children when it is the right time. I'm going to buy my own house. In addition, I will give my testimony at churches to teenagers, so they won't go through what I have. (Mauricio's journal)

During the interviews, I asked Mauricio to read and reflect about what he wrote when he was still my student. It was evident that he showed a level of frustration and guilt. He said,

Cuando escribí eso pensé que eso era lo que iba a hacer el resto de mi vida, pero ahora me di cuenta que no, pero trajo consecuencias. Me salí (de la universidad), me endeudé y ahora tengo que trabajar para pagar y poder estudiar lo que quiero.

When I wrote it, I thought that it was what I was going to do for the rest of my life, but now I have realized that no, but it brought consequences. I dropped out (of college) and had a debt and now I have to work to pay that back and continue my studies, which is what I want.

Mauricio received financial aid to pursue higher education and since he dropped out, he realized that he needed to pay his loan back. By the time I interviewed him, he was working at a mattress factory and getting ready to start attending a private barber school. His goal was to pay his loan back and quit his current job, so he could become a full-time barber student.

After Luz finished high school, she started attending a local community college part-time. She took online courses since she was also working full-time at a factory. During her second year of college, she got sick and was hospitalized for a couple of weeks, pushing her to miss class time. When the end of the semester came, she was not allowed to take her finals since she had missed many days of school. After that, she decided to drop out of college. She shared,

> Me dolió mucho que mis récords decía que todo ese semestre aparecía reprobado porque había faltado esas dos semanas y había llevado mi record médico y todo y no me lo aceptaron.

> *It hurt me a lot that my transcripts showed that I had failed the whole semester because I had missed two week and although I took medical documentation, they did not accept it.*

After five years, Luz decided to return to college, but her biggest obstacle was her immigration status in the country and lack of financial government support to qualify as in-state students. Pérez (2012) claims that undocumented students usually question the idea of meritocracy when they realize that although they are committed to their education through hard work, they have fewer opportunities compared to their U.S. born peers. Luz commented,

> Intenté regresar pero lo que me detenía era no tener ayuda financiera. Por no ser legal me rechazaron porque yo no podía recibir ningún tipo de ayuda. Como los papeles de mi papá no eran legales, él no podía ayudarme. Mis tres hermanos sí tenemos seguro pero eso solo era para estudiar y sí me sirvió para el colegio porque yo pagaba in-state-tuition pero no aplicaba para FAFSA.

> *I tried to go back, but what stopped me was not having financial aid. Since I was not legal, they rejected me because I could not get any type of financial support. Since my father's papers were not legal, he could not help me. My three siblings and I have a social security number but just for studying and it helped me to attend college because I used it to pay in-state-tuition but could not apply for FAFSA.*

Sofia and Esperanza were still pursuing higher education when I interviewed then in 2017. Sofia's dream about attending college was challenged when she realized that she needed to pay out-of-state tuition due to her immigration status in the U.S. (Pérez, 2012). She said,

> Me gradué en el 2009. Después del 2009 yo quise ir a inscribirme al RCC, pero cuando yo fuí allí me dijeron que yo tenía que pagar el triple de lo que era y luego de eso que no tenía seguro social. Yo no podía estudiar, entonces me decidí meterme a trabajar full-time en McDonald's y ya me quedé trabajando. Me ofrecieron el puesto de manager. Seguí trabajando por dos años. Después de dos años como manager quise volver a intentar lo de la escuela y me dijeron no por no tener seguro.

I graduated in 2009. After 2009, I wanted to register at RCC, but when I went there, I was told that I had to pay three times more since I did not have social security. I could not study, then I decided to start working full-time at McDonald's and I stayed there. I was offered a manager position. I continued working for two years. After two years as manager, I wanted to try at the community college and was told that I could not do it due to my lack of a social security number.

Like Sofia and Esperanza, many undocumented Latinx students who benefit through DACA realize that they can pursue higher education at local community colleges; however, they cannot qualify to get federal loans due to their immigration status. Pérez (2012) states that, "Balancing school and work becomes very difficult for students who must take on full-time jobs to earn enough money to pay for their tuition" (p. 30). However, those who decide to fulfill their dreams end up paying out-of-state tuition. Those who decide to drop out, prefer to start working to support their parents or start their own families.

Like Sofia, few students become resilient and decide to challenge the system. When she had her son, she happened to know about DACA and decided to apply. She shared,

En el año 2011 salió el programa de DACA. Apliqué para DACA y ya me calificaron. Gracias a Dios agarré mi permiso de trabajo. Agarré otra promoción en la compañía donde estaba trabajando. Fuí, apliqué al community college para regresar a estudiar y me aceptaron. Empecé el semestre online. Hice ese semestre. No quise tomar mucho porque el cargo que ya estaba teniendo en la tienda donde trabajaba, yo sentí que me iba a estresar, que no iba poder con la escuela, el trabajo, el niño. Pensé que se me iba a ser muy difícil. Por eso hasta ahorita lo que estoy haciendo es tomando una clase por semestre, para no descuidar ni la escuela, ni el trabajo, ni el niño. La clase es online. Estoy en el tercer semestre estudiando business administration.

In 2011, DACA program started. I applied to DACA and got qualified. Thank God I was given a work permit. I accepted my job promotion. I applied to the community college to go back to school and was accepted. I started the semester online. I finished that semester. I did not want to take many courses because with my new position at work. I did not want to be stressed. I thought that I would not be able to handle school, work, and my child. I thought it was going to be very difficult. That's why I am currently taking one course per semester, so I won't neglect school, work, and the child. The course is online. I am on my third semester, studying business administration.

It is important to highlight about Sofia's hard work ethics. Since she was my student, she always showed commitment to better herself as one of the main reasons why she left her grandmother, who was like her mother, behind in El Salvador. Being a single mother with a full-time job required a lot from her, but her resiliency came now from her son and his future. By the time I interviewed her, she was thinking about moving back with her parents, so her mom could help her take care of her son.

Like Sofia, Elisa's college experience was not easy at all. First, she learned how to navigate college basically by herself, overcoming language and academic barriers. After completing her associate degree, she decided to transfer to a four-year university in the area. She shared,

> Well, after I finished high school, I went straight to (community college) to get my associate degree there so I could transfer to another university, so it was cheaper (cheaper). So, I finished that. I got my associate degree and then I transferred to (university) to study fashion design. When I was studying fashion design, I went to the (community college) and got my certificate in wedding and planning directing, so I have been involved in studying when I can. So now I am two semesters behind to graduate, to finish my two classes and then I finish my undergraduate in fashion design.

When I interviewed Esperanza, she was a junior at a private university in North Carolina. Through the interview, she shared how much she regretted not having a mentor or counselor at her high school who could have advised her to take college prep courses that could transfer to college. Pérez (2012) suggests that having a positive school-based relationship allows adolescents to have guidance and support and to gain access to relevant information about college and how to apply for it. Also, she felt overwhelmed while getting used to college expectations. She shared,

> I went right away to (local community college) for three years because I kept changing my major and I dropped a lot of classes that I was afraid of taking, I was just too scared that I was gonna fail them and it was just too much for me since my language wasn't that great.

> Yes, I was struggling through those classes trying to take math, calculus, and math in college and I just could not do; it was too hard and I reduced the number of class that I had to take 'cause I was supposed to take 15 classes each semester but I only took ten or twelve and then I didn't really know what I wanted to do. I didn't. I wish there was somebody there like to help me what kind of class I need to take and what is transferring in and what is not transferring in. I kinda regret it, like I said I wish there was somebody like pushing me like through like "you need to take these classes, this one transfer in, or that" and now I'm just I wish I had talked to somebody and I mean I would graduate right now if I had pushed it through for four years, so yeah (thinking) is a regret big time, but yeah, here I am. I feel like (laughing) like I am too old to graduate from college right now, but I guess is not.

Last time I got in touch with Esperanza, she was still attending a private university. After changing majors, she was finally graduating in May 2020. It is important to highlight Esperanza's resilience to remain in college. After being through many life obstacles with her relatives once in the U.S. and being adopted by her foster mother (a White and Christian woman), she also had to fight other social obstacles while in school due to the fact that even though she looked like a stereotypical Latina, she was not able to communicate in Spanish since she belonged to a Mayan tribe from Guatemala. In order to survive all of these personal and social hurdles, Esperanza needed to learn English to excel academically and Spanish to develop a sense of racial/ethnic belonging. It is important to highlight that her biggest support came from her foster mother whose social capital and agency allowed her to fulfill her college education.

Gloria and Julio moved back to México and ended up attending and graduating from college. Gloria's decision to go back to her country by herself showed a high level of perseverance and commitment. I still recall when she called me over the phone to let me know that she was on her way to México to pursue college. Through social media, we were able to stay in contact with each other. In the summer of 2017, Gloria was visiting her parents after finishing her university studies. She knew through Luz that I was in town interviewing some of my other students as part of my study. She willingly volunteered to be part of it. When I asked her about her life after completing high school and pursue college, she said,

> Cuando terminé la high school me enfoqué a trabajar directamente en una casa de empeño como administradora. Mi idea era siempre estudiar, sobresalir. Me dije Estados Unidos no lo voy a poder lograr porque no tengo los documentos. Decidí trabajar dos años para poder pagar una parte de mi carrera he irme a México. En México fue muy difícil. Ya no era ni de aquí ni de allá porque ya tenía rasgos de Estados Unidos. En México me costó mucho tener que estar escribiendo en español debido pues a los acentos, las comas, los puntos. Me costó mucho trabajo con la letra G y J para poder escribir correctamente y más por la carrera que había tomado, comunicación. Me costó mucho trabajo.

> *When I finished high school, I focused on working as a manager at a pawn shop. My goal was always to study, stand out. I said to myself, I will not do it in the United States because I don't have legal papers. I decided to work for two years to pay part of my education and then go back to México. In México, it was very difficult since I was not from here nor there since I had already assimilated the United States culture. In México, it took me a lot to write in Spanish when using accent marks, commas, periods. I took me a long time with the letters G and J. In order to write correctly and even more for the career that I had taken, communications. It took me a lot of work.*

Like Esperanza, Gloria's counternarrative talks about resilience and hard work. First, she decided to work and save some money to pursue her dream of attending college in México. She shared about her difficulties while getting used to standard

Spanish since she has been used to the English language. Besides relearning her mother tongue and getting used to college at a private institution, Gloria learned to advocate and protect herself away from her parents and two younger brothers, who stayed in North Carolina. She shared how she had to get up and go to bed early as part of her college policies and rules. However, she graduated in 2014 with a bachelor's in communication and media.

Like most undocumented Latinx students in the U.S., Francisco, Diana, Antonio, and Dulce could not pursue higher education due to their immigration status, lack of financial support, and agency. Pérez (2012) argues that undocumented students who attend community college face significant challenges since they do not qualify to benefit from federal financial support. Many of them have to work to pay for their school expenses and to support their parents financially. Francisco shared,

> Uno piensa que saliendo de la high school ya lo logró, pero no es así. Tienes que seguir estudiando si quieres lograr algo, algo que te pueda respaldar para el resto de tu vida. Yo intenté entrar al RCC pero desafortunadamente en ese tiempo no ganaba mucho y mi mamá no tenía mucho trabajo, so era difícil tener los recursos para pagar todo ese dinero. Por no tener papeles tienes que pagar más dinero. Intenté aplicar al DACA pero no se logró porque cuando yo llegué aquí fue como a finales de enero y yo cumplí 16 años el 14 de enero (takes a deep breath). Lo dejé ya cosas del destino. Algo pasa porque yo intenté demasiadas veces y gasté mucho dinero con abogados.

> *One thinks that after graduating from high school, you are done, but it is not that way. You have to continue studying if you want to accomplish something, something that back support you for the rest of your life. I tried to enter RCC, but unfortunately, during that time I did not make a lot of money and my mom did not have a job, so it was very difficult to have the resources to pay all of that money. If you do not have papers, you have to pay more money. I tried DACA but did not qualify because when I came here, it was by the end of January and I turned 16 January 14. I left the rest to destiny (resilience). Something happened because I tried many times and spent a lot of money on lawyers.*

Juan Ríos: ¿Qué pasó después que te graduaste de la high school?

Juan Ríos: What happened after high school graduation?

Francisco: Seguí en McDonald's, traté de seguir creciendo en el campo de manager y seguir ascendiendo. Todo iba bien hasta que pasó. Creo que una persona que estaba ahí la investigaron, y pues por una empezaron a investigar a todos. No solo fuí yo, fueron muchísimos que estaban conmigo, managers también y los liquidaron a todos, como unos 10 o 15 más o menos. Y muchos perdieron su trabajo. Habían personas que dependían de su trabajo. Tenían familias. Hicieron como una auditoría, un abogado de ellos y la de recursos humanos empezaron a hacerte preguntas, "¿Desde cuándo llegaste aquí? ¿Cómo obtuviste tus documentos? y todo?" Como ya teniendo todo en la mesa, entiende? Ya que puede uno hacer. Solo querían escucharlo de ti. Me tocó la de mala. Estaba ya como gerente y ganaba como de 500 a 600 por semana. Todo pasa por algo.

Francisco: I continued at McDonald's. I tried to grow in the managerial field, going up. Everything was fine until that happened. I think a person that was under investigation and then started checking on everybody (immigration status). I was not the only one. There were a lot that were with me, managers too and they laid us off, like 10 or 15 more less. And many of them lost their jobs. There were people who depended on their jobs. There were families. They did an audit, their lawyer and human resources people started to ask us questions, "When did you start working here? How did you get your documents? And everything." Like setting everything it up, you know. One could not do anything. They just wanted to hear it from you. It was my bad luck. I was a manager and used to earn 500 or 600 per week. Things happen for a reason.

Francisco's narratives talk about resilience and hope. Although he worked very hard in high school to learn the new language and to take advanced courses, his biggest barrier was when he realized that he could not benefit from DACA since he came to the U.S. after he turned sixteen. Although he spent a lot of money with immigration attorneys to submit his DACA papers, he was not able to qualify. Then when he tried to pursue higher education at a local community college, he was told that he had to pay out-of-state tuition since he did not have legal immigration documents to be in the U.S. Additionally, he was laid off from work after being asked about his legal status. Francisco's resilience and hope come from his sense of responsibility to support his mother and younger brother, a U.S. citizen. He shared with me that his goal is to give his mother back for what she did for him and his siblings when they were back in México.

Similarly, Dulce's narrative about her goals to pursue higher education become unobtainable when she realized that due to her immigration status and not being able to qualify for DACA, she was not able to attend college.

JR: ¿Qué pasó después que te graduaste de la high school?

JR: What happened after you graduated from high school?

Dulce: Seguir trabajando. Quería reunir dinero para seguir estudiando pero ya no seguí.

Dulce: I continued working. I wanted to save some money to continue my education, I didn't do it.

JR: ¿Porqué?

JR: Why?

Dulce: No sé. Era más fácil estar en casa y ayudar a mis papás que estudiar. Al no tener papeles, la educación es más cara. Intenté ir al college, pero no me inscribí. Bueno tal vez uno se deja llevar por lo que dicen de que era muy difícil, muy caro. Mi mamá quería que yo estudiara y dejara de trabajar. Ella me iba a pagar los estudios, pero a mí no se me hizo justo que mi mamá se sacrificara por mi y decidí no estudiar.

Dulce: I don't know. It was easier to stay home and help my parents than to study. Since I didn't have papers, education is more expensive. I tried to attend college, but I didn't regis-ter. Well, maybe one pays more attention to what people tell you that college is very difficult, very expensive. My mother wanted me to study instead of working. She wanted to pay for my studies, but I found it unfair that my mom had to sacrifice herself for me, so I decided not to study.

JR: ¿Y decidiste trabajar tiempo completo?

JR: and you decided to work full-time?

Dulce: De por sí ya trabajaba tiempo completo. Trabajaba en el mismo lugar que cuando estudiaba. Operaba una máquina. Cuando empecé a trabajar ayudaba a recibir el producto que salía, pero como empecé a llevarme con los operadores y despidieron a un americano. A los pocos meses me dieron el puesto porque aprendí rápido.

Ganaba como $8.50 la hora. Trabajaba por hora y me pagaban por semana alrededor de $300.00 por semana. Desafortunadamente no me pude beneficiar del DACA por la edad que tenía cuando llegué.

Dulce: Well, I used to work full-time anyway. I used to work while I was attending high school. I used to operate a machine. When I started to work, I used to help to receive the fin-ished product, but since I started getting along with other machine operators and they laid off an American man. After a few months, they offered me his position because I learned fast.

Diana's narrative is very similar to Dulce's. I realized that most undocumented Latinx students lacked reliable sources of information about college admission and fees. Some found it was too expensive for them. Instead, most of them decided to find jobs in factories, construction, and fast-food restaurants while others decided to start their own families.

Tenía planes de ir a la universidad, pero el problema era que yo era indocumentada. Quise ir a uno (college) de Charlotte para estudiar cosmetología, pero la información que yo estaba buscando, me pedían los documentos. Me cerraron las puertas de una vez. Yo no tenía documentos, so si ahí en un colegio no me permitian por mis docu-mentos, pues en donde me lo iban a permitir. So no, me quedé así.

I had plans to attend college, but the problem was that I was undocumented. I wanted to attend college in Charlotte to study cosmetology, but the information that I was looking for asked for legal documents. They closed the doors at me right away. I didn't have documents, so if college did not allow me to study because of my documents, well there was no other place that would allow me to continue my education. So, I did not go.

Antonio's narrative about pursuing college is a little bit different from Francisco and Dulce. Although he benefited from DACA, he decided not to pursue higher education since he was told that he had to pay out-of-state tuition. He said,

> DACA no te ayuda para pagar in-state-tuition. Todavía sigue siendo como si no tuvieras papeles porque te cobran como si vinieran de afuera lo cual es el doble o el triple de lo que un local paga.

> *DACA doesn't help you to pay in-state-tuition. It still feels like if you don't have papers because you are charged as if you came from abroad, which is double, or triple compared to what a local pay.*

Different from other undocumented Latinx students Antonio did not have the navigational capital to realize that students who qualified for DACA were able to attend some local community colleges in North Carolina and pay in-state-tuition. Instead, he went by what he heard from relatives and friends about college fees for undocumented students.

Documented and undocumented Latinx students find themselves ill-equipped to pursue higher education. Some of them have the best intentions to make dreams come true of becoming positive role models and professionals to support their parents and relatives living in the U.S. and back in their homelands. Unfortunately, all of those dreams become out of reach once they start attending community colleges. Few of them, like Esperanza and Elisa, learn to navigate the college system through challenging academic and psychological hurdles. Others, like Francisco and Mauricio, cannot resist a colorblind and racist system decide to drop out that make many Latinx students feel invisible and discriminated. Finally, most undocumented Latinx students do not further their higher education due to the fact that they do not qualify for DACA, lack of financial support from the federal government and their parents. In the next section, I explore the narratives of Antonio and Dulce, whose narratives about being Latinx and undocumented intersect their sexual orientation as gay and lesbian, respectively.

New Families and Jobs

It is a fact that college is not for everyone. Due to a poor K-12 education, financial problems, family responsibilities, or immigration status in this country, many Latinx individuals decide to start their new families or to get jobs after they finish high school. In this section, I analyze Diana's and Sofia's new families. I discuss how Dulce and Antonio become resilient after finding low-wage and risky jobs. Finally, I talk about Luz's moral obligation to give back to her parents.

When I interviewed Diana, she showed up to the library with her husband and two beautiful children (a girl and a boy). It was interesting to realize that

Diana had already spoken to her husband about me and my study. After introducing myself to Diana's husband, he took the children to the children's section of the library, so I could interview her. When I asked her about her life after high school, she told me that her parents wanted her to stay home to help her mother around the house. I recalled that when I first met Diana, I realized that her parents were very strict, and her father used to be a pastor in a Spanish-speaking Christian church. I also learned that Diana did not get along with her mother. I felt that Diana never forgave her parents for leaving her behind in Honduras to move to the U.S. Diana looked very content with her new family. She was a full-time and stay-at-home mother.

> Ahorita estoy cuidando a mis niños. Tomé la decisión de primero de casarme, tener mi niña, de hecho yo quería quedarme solo con mi niña, pero esperé que mi niña creciera un poco por lo menos a que ella fuera a kinder o pre-k para yo sentirme más confiada que ella va a estar cierto tiempo en la escuela y yo poder estar trabajando sin poder estar preocupando porque soy muy desconfiada de dejar mis hijos con (extraños). Mi hija tiene cinco años, el niño tiene uno. Y yo tenía el plan ya que mi niña comenzara la escuela, yo iba a buscarme un trabajo más o menos como un part-time para yo ir guardando un poco para la carrera que yo quiero tomar, pero mi niña como a los cuatro años se volvió muy insistente de que quería tener un hermano, so ella cambió mis planes. Yo soy una persona que yo prefiero mi familia. Siento que tengo más tiempo, estoy joven. Tengo 27 años, pero tengo metas.

> *Right now, I'm taking care of my children. I made the decision to get married first, to have my daughter. By the way, I only wanted to have my daughter, but I waited until my daughter was ready to start kindergarten or pre-k so I could feel more confident about her staying in school and I could be working without being worried since I don't trust my children to strangers. My daughter is five years. The boy is one. And I had a plan since my daughter was about to start school. I was going to find me a job, like a part-time, so I could start saving money for the career I wanted to study, but when my daughter was four years, she insisted that she wanted to have a brother, so she changed my plans (laughing). I am a person who prefers a family. I feel that I have more time. I am still young. I am 27 years, but I have goals.*

Although Diana did not pursue college due to a lack of support from her parents and knowledge about DACA, she decided to start her own family without her parents' will. She shared with me how she needed to move away from her parents' house to live with some friends from church to date her children's father. During the interview, Diana showed a sense of fulfillment as a woman, wife, and mother. She shared with me that she did not matter to sacrifice her future goals. Instead, she preferred to spend more time with her children, contrary to what her parents did to her when they left her back in Honduras when they decided to immigrate to the U.S.

Sofia's busy life revolves around her full-time job as a manager at a fast-food restaurant, her son, and her online courses at a local community college. She shared with me how hard her days are. She said,

Bueno, al principio sí no quería estudiar, no quería estudiar porque yo pensaba que si yo me metía a estudiar yo iba a descuidar al niño. No quería estudiar porque yo decía va ser mucho, luego el trabajo, la escuela. No voy este poder con todo y la primera semana sí, cuando decidí ir a inscribirme me fue muy difícil la primera semana porque yo sentía que no estaba dedicándole tiempo al estudio, que no le estaba dedicando tiempo al niño, que no le estaba dedicando tiempo a mi trabajo. Lo que tuve que hacer fue sentarme y ponerme a organizar mis cosas, mis rutinas, que días iba a dedicarle a la escuela, que dia iba a dedicarme para hacer mis tareas nada más organizarme porque yo puedo ir online y hacer mis cosas cuando el niño está en la escuela; mis días de descanso, descanso entre semana un día y los domingos. Trabajo los sábados en la mañana.

Well, at the beginning I didn't want to study, I didn't want to study because I thought that if I started to study, it would be too much, then work and school. I thought I couldn't handle it and the first week yes, when I decided to register, it was very difficult during the first week because I felt that I was focusing more on my studies, that I was not paying attention to my son, that I was not paying attention to my job. I sat down and got organized my things, my routines, which days I was going to study, what days I was going to do my homework. It was a matter of getting organized because I can be online and still do my things when my son is in school. My days off. I rest one day during the week and Sundays. I work on Saturday mornings.

Sofia's hectic life as a full-time worker and mom keep her focused on her goals to complete her college career and to take care of her child. As a single mother, she has learned to be very organized; however, she still gets some support from her parents who live close by. She spent some time talking about her typical day.

Un día típico mío. Levantarme, andar correteando a mi niño que se arregle, que se prepare para ir a la escuela, llevarlo a la escuela, irme yo a trabajar, regresar de la escuela, ir con mi mamá para que me dé el niño, hablar con el niño, que hizo, que le gustó, que es lo que no le gustó, que es lo que haría diferente. Dependiendo de cómo fue su día, vamos a agarrar un ice cream, vamos al parque, vamos a la tienda. Hacemos cualquier cosa dependiendo de cómo él haiga hecho en ese día. Luego de eso, si me toca ir a la church. Luego regresamos a la casa, o vamos a comer si tengo que hacer mi tarea, la hago.

A typical day for me. I get up and have to run after my son, so he can get ready to go to school. I take him to school. Then I go to work, come back from school, go to my Mom so she can take care of my son, talk to my son, ask him what he did in school, what he liked, what he didn't like, what he would do differently. Depending on how his day went, then we go to eat ice cream, go to the park, go shopping. We do anything, depending on how he has done on that day. Then we go to church. Then we come back home or go to eat out and if I have homework to do, I do it.

Although I never asked questions about her child's father, she shared with me taking him to court to fill out child support documentation and shared visits. She commented,

> Estuvimos en corte por el proceso del niño por el child support y ahorita sí estamos negociando en el que él esté mas presente con el niño, pero no vive el niño con él, ni hasta ni lo ve diariamente. Él es americano. Fue buen papá cuando recien nacido el niño, pero después que el niño nació, al año fue una persona diferente. En el aspecto a que él se acompañó otra vez (got a new partner). Al año que el niño tenía el año, se juntó con otra persona y esa persona no le permitía que estuviera cerca del niño. Entonces en ese tiempo si el empezó a cambiar más con el niño. Ya tenía que decirle ven a ver a tu hijo.

> *We went to court to follow up child support and right now we are negotiating that he needs to spend more time with his son. My son doesn't live with and he doesn't see him daily. He's American. He used to be a good Dad when my son was born, but then after that, after a year, he became a different person. He has a new girlfriend. After my child turned one, he moved him with another person and that person didn't allow him to be around his son. Since then, he started changing with my son. I had to tell him to come and see your son.*

Even though Sofia has faced a lot of obstacles while immigrating to this country, at school, and after, she never gave up. Her son gives her HOPE and resilience to move on in life. Later, I learned that she is an active member of a Christian church and had a new boyfriend.

Antonio lives and works in retail in a larger city in North Carolina. He considers himself being independent from his mother and two brothers. When I asked how his life had changed after high school, he said,

> Ha cambiado en la forma de independizarme de mi familia. El idioma más que bien lo sigo aprendiendo, pero lo poco que aprendí ahí me ayuda a diario con el trato de personas y me desenvuelvo más con más facilidad. Ya no tengo tanto miedo de decir o de investigar algo. Tenía miedo antes porque las personas se burlaban de mi acento. En vez de ayudarme, o porque las personas siempre que yo trataba de explicarme con ellos, con los maestros sus frases siempre eran, "Oh, no sabes inglés y ya. Está bien". Entonces en vez de ayudarme a abrirme más me hacían sentir mal. Eso me da menos motivos para hablarlo, desenvolverme más porque era tanto miedo de que se iban a burlar de mí. En ese momento me sentía que no pertenecía a los Estados Unidos, que estaba simplemente en un lugar equivocado. Ahora me siento más cómodo porque se el idioma, no tanto, pero puedo defenderme y me siento como cualquier otra persona. Tengo lo básico (idioma) para ir a mi trabajo y desenvolverse y vivir un día normal como una persona nacida aquí. Simplemente lo único que nos diferencia es el acento y un estatus legal.

> *I have become independent from my family. I keep on learning the language, but the little that I learned allows me to talk to people and I can speak it easily. I'm not afraid to say or to*

find out something. I used to be afraid because people used to make fun of my accent. Instead of helping me o because people always that I tried to explain myself, with teachers, their phrases were, "Oh, you don't know English, and ok. That's fine." Then instead of supporting me to open up and talk, they made me feel bad. It used to give me less reasons to talk, to manage myself even more because I was afraid that people would make fun of me. At that moment, I felt that I did not belong to the United States. That I was simply in the wrong place. Now, I feel more comfortable because I can speak the language, not that much, but I can advocate for myself and I feel like any other person. I have the basic (language) to go to work and make myself understood and to live a normal day like somebody who was born here.

Me: ¿De qué trabajas ahora?

Me: What kind of job do you know now?

Antonio: Vendía ropa, bueno lo sigo haciendo, pero ahora tengo una posición de manager. Me mudé a (new city) hace tres meses. Siempre me he considerado independizado porque siempre he trabajado. Yo vivía fuera de mi casa ya en (town's name). Yo vivía en un apartamento solo.

Antonio: I used to sell clothing, well I still do it, but I have a managerial position now. I moved (to a new city) three months ago. I have always considered myself independent because I have always worked. I used to live by myself in (town's name). I used to live in an apartment alone.

Moving away from home not only allows Antonio to become independent from his mom and two brothers, but it allows him to live his sexuality. Being away from his relatives has pushed him to learn how to advocate for himself and how to better himself to build his own agency. During our last interview, Antonio shared with me some pictures of him dressed in drag. He told me how much he enjoyed doing drag queen shows sometimes on weekends.

One of the most relevant issues that Latinx immigrants experience in the U.S. is the fact that getting a high school diploma is not enough to experience upper ladder social mobility (Irizarry, 2011; Noguera, Hurtado, & Fergus, 2013; Ríos Vega, 2015; Valenzuela,1999). Research studies have proved that Latinx students who graduate from high school end up doing the same type of jobs than those immigrants who never attended school in the U.S. After graduating from high school, Dulce decided not to attend college since she found it too expensive and Luz dropped out of college due to medical and family moral responsibilities. As a result, both ended working in factories, joining their relatives and friends.

Dulce's job

Me levanto a las seis y me voy al trabajo a las seis y media y entro al trabajo a las siete. No tengo horario de salida. A veces salgo a las cinco, a las seis. Trabajo por producción. Tengo que ganar cierta cantidad y mi producción se basa en el trabajo que hago en el día. Me pagan por semana. En una semana cuando el trabajo está bajo, sacamos con cuatro ciento cincuenta y cuando sacamos muchas órdenes, sacamos hasta ochocientos dólares por semana.

I get up at six and go to work at six thirty. And start working at seven. I don't have an exact hour to leave hour. Sometimes, it is a five, six. I work based on production. I earn a certain amount of money and my production is based on the type of job that I do during the day. I get paid weekly. In a week, when the production is low, I make four hundred fifty and when they have a lot of demand, we can make eight hundred dollars in a week.

Luz's job

Es una compañía que se llama Princess House. Entras como una consultante y después de ahí subes a diferentes niveles. Yo tengo un grupo ya un poco grande ... y entonces lo que me toca a mi es asegurarme que ese grupo vaya bien.

It's a company called Princess House. You start as a consultant and then you go up different levels. I have a large group and then my job is to make sure my group is doing fine.

It was not to my surprise to hear some of my former students share how they did not mind sacrificing their future lives to pay their parents back for all they did to either raise them or to bring them to the U.S. Francisco, Dulce, and Luz shared similar stories of giving back to their parents. By the time I interviewed Dulce and Luz, they were working on production at local factories. Luz shared,

Mi meta es juntar un poco de dinero para que el día de mañana mis papás ya no tengan que trabajar cuando ya estén grandes. Así que buscar la manera de yo ayudarlos. Eso también es lo que me ayuda a seguir.

My goal is to save some money, so one day my parents won't work when they get older. I will find a way to support them. That also pushes me to continue.

Similar to Dulce's attitude about sacrificing their futures to pay their parents back. Luz talked about her parents' health and her sense of responsibility for being single.

Su salud (her mother) ha ido empeorando y por mucho tiempo ella estuvo en el hospital con diabetes. Le dejaron de funcionar los riñones. Entonces eso me impidió de yo seguir estudiando porque me enfoque más en ella y en ayudar en los gastos de casa. Me sentía obligada moralmente. Y también a mi padre le dió como un derrame y él no pudo trabajar por mucho tiempo, por más de un año, y también ya está un poco de edad y ya no consigue trabajo tan fácilmente como una persona joven. Siento que aunque yo haga mi vida, tengo que ver todo lo que ellos hicieron por mí. Yo pienso que estaría mal si yo los dejara o los abandonara porque yo sé que ellos ocupan de mí. He dejado de hacer muchas cosas por estar allí con ellos.

Her health has worsened, and she was in the hospital with diabetes. Her kidneys stopped working. Then it didn't allow me to continue my studies because I focused on her and helped

her cover the house expenses. I felt obliged morally speaking. And my Dad had a stroke and he could not work for a long time, more than a year, and he was also getting older and could not get a job so easily like a young person could. I feel that although I start my own family, I have to thank them for all they did for me. I feel that it would be wrong if I left or abandoned them because they took care of me. I have stopped doing a lot of things to be here with them.

Last time I heard from Dulce she was working on construction. She was no longer living and dating the Mexican woman she introduced me as her partner. Luz was still working at a factory and taking care of her sick parents.

Being a Latinx student represents multiple challenges in education. In the U.S., Latinx students realize that their skin color, Spanish accent in English, and gender make them the perfect target to be discriminated against or to become invisible to mainstream society, usually Whites. What happens to undocuqueers like Dulce and Antonio who suffer double discrimination. First, from their own kind due to their sexual orientation. Second, they are discriminated and oppressed by society due to their ethnicity, immigration status, and gender. In the next section, I discuss how my former students' broken dreams also encouraged them to become resilient and to find HOPE and understand that things will get better in the future.

Broken Dreams and Resilience

No fue muy corto pero fue el que más se me hace a mí (prompted) sé que no pude cumplirlo porque ya no pude estudiar pero eso nunca me ha quitado en mente de que lo voy a lograr. Yo sigo intentando.

It was very short, but what bothers me is that I could not accomplish it because I could not study, but it is still in my mind that will do it. I keep trying. (Francisco)

I asked Francisco to reflect on all of his plans while he was in school compared to where he is now. He talked about how much he appreciates his mother's efforts and hard work, so he wants to pay her back with his work. He said,

El que más me llama la atención son los planes que uno hace y uno quiero pero que a veces como que … se te cierran las puertas … Por ejemplo cuando hablaba del trabajo de mi mama, yo sabía todo lo que ella había pasado por nosotros, que ha sido madre soltera y siempre ha luchado por nosotros y quizás ella no pudo rehacer su vida por siempre estar trabajando y siempre buscando el pan de cada día para nosotros y mis hermanas en México, so yo quería seguir estudiando y conseguir un trabajo para que ella no tuviera que seguir trabajando para un patrón.

What caught my attention the most were the plans that we make and want, but sometimes like doors get closed. For instance, when I used to talk about my Mom's job, I knew all the things that she had to go through for us, that she had been a single mother and had always

fought for us and maybe she could never remarried since she was always working and always looking for food for us and my sisters in México every day, so I wanted to continue my studies and get a job, so she did not have to continue working for somebody else.

Although Francisco's dreams to pursue higher education were broken due to his immigration status and lack of financial support as undocumented, he still found resilience by helping his Mother and younger brother. His goal was to support his Mother with his hard work. As the only male adult in his house, he felt a moral obligation to protect and to advocate for his Mother and younger brother. Francisco also talked about opening a family business as his new goal. He shared,

Ahorita lo que estoy haciendo es ahorrando y como ya no pude pero no es porque no quise sino porque este tuve demasiadas contras y fue un poco más difícil de tener oportunidad de entrar a la escuela. Pero la meta ahorita es ahorrar y poner un negocio familiar de comida. El plan es que si ya no se pudo con lo que quería de cierta manera tratar de hacer la vida más fácil ya no como antes. Pero desde hace tiempo ya ella (his mom) no trabaja. Está en la casa ya que no había trabajo. Yo le dije que ya no se preocupara porque yo siempre estoy para ayudarla.

Now, I am saving some money and it wasn't like I didn't want to do it, but I had a lot of obstacles against me and it was difficult to have the opportunity to pursue higher education. But my goal now is to save some money and start a family food business. The plan is that if it didn't work one way as I wanted, I will try to make life easier than before. It has been a while since my Mom doesn't work. She's at home since there were no jobs available. I told her not be worried because I was always going to be there to support her.

By the time I interviewed Francisco, he was working with some relatives in construction after he was laid off from his last job after it was audited and discovered that many employees were undocumented. Similar to Francisco's narrative, Dulce was working in construction. Before her last job, she worked at a furniture factory. She said,

Ahí primero entré a un área que le llaman backfield que es donde se rellenan todos los muebles y se les da forma. Ahí estaba por producción. Teníamos que trabajar muy rápido. Después me pasaron al área de *kits* donde se separa todo el material que va a los diferentes departamentos. Y después estuve en Winston igual en el backfield, pero ya era yo allí este líder. Estaba un poco buena la paga. Era por producción.

There, first you start in an area called backfield, which is where they fill out all furniture and shape. I used to work on production. We had to work very fast. Then they sent me to the kits area where you take apart all the materials that go to different departments. And then I was in Winston in the backfield again, but over there, I was a leader. They paid me better there. It was based on production.

When I asked her how she felt about seeing other students who dropped out of school doing the same type of job she was doing. She said,

> "Estudia", decía mi madre. (laughing). "Eso es lo único que pienso". Que debí haber seguido estudiando y no estar así. No tiene nada de malo el trabajo, pero pude haber hecho algo mejor.

> Es difícil. Pues uno quiere ser mejor (tears in her eyes). Esa no es la vida que yo hubiese querido en México. Yo siempre mi meta fue estudiar, pero aquí no pude. No pude hacer nada y si duele. (crying). Se siente bien feo.

> *"Study," my Mom used to tell me (laughing). "That's the only thing I want you to do." I should have continued studying instead of being like this. My job is not bad, but I could have done something better. It's difficult. One wants to become better (tears in her eyes). That is not the life that I had wanted in México. I goal was always to study, but I couldn't do it here. I could not do anything, and it hurts (crying). It feels very bad.*

Dulce has always been a strong woman. Since she was my student, she always had big dreams to become an engineer in the future. She always behaved more mature than the rest of the students in class. Before she finished high school, she was already working and had bought her first car. She took her younger siblings to school every day. Like Francisco and Luz, Dulce also developed a sense of responsibility to pay her parents back for they did for her and to take care of them when they were not able to work anymore.

Sofia's resiliency was evident when I asked her to compare her high school and college experiences. She said,

> I had to do a lot of writing, of course. I did it in high school, but it wasn't the same, it was higher education and sometimes I was working at (fast food restaurant). By that time, I used to get out at eleven o'clock at night and go straight home to do homework and sometime I used to be up until 5 am to get up at seven and get ready to go to school, but it was hard because I didn't know how to pronounce things and how to translate it, because almost everyone knows that we think in Spanish and then we have to translate and it was hard, it was hard. And we have a writing center, but it wasn't the same. I thought a lot about quitting college. But then I read that I needed to keep going. Because I'm not as most of the kids decide to drop out or quit because of something else. My parents motivated me to keep on going. Because they don't know English. That was frustrating when we had the (high school) meeting with parents and of course you were there to translate and but they are uneducated so they can't work with a higher wage or anything, so yeah they were my strength to keep going and support them as they did when I was little.

One of the most eye-opening things that I experienced that I had through my interviews with Sofia was her "orgullo" (pride) to prove mainstream society that not all Latinx students were the same. Throughout our conversations, I witnessed how she thanked her parents for sacrificing themselves to bring her and her sib-lings to the U.S. She talked about how hard her father had to work to pay for her college and books. Also, she talked about her long hours working at a fast-food restaurant even when was still in high school.

Julio's resiliency story is a little bit different since he did not complete high school in the U.S. Instead, he had no choice but to sign self-deportation after breaking the law. However, I always kept his journal since he was always a good writer. I lost contact with him for many years. I did not know what had happened to him until I finally found him on Facebook. We reconnected after ten years. When I talked to him about my book project and his journal, he immediately volunteered to support me. After he shared with me the reasons why he moved back to México, I was happy to know about his education in México. He shared,

> So I finished high school, I finished my technical career on auto mechanic. When I started working at that place, over here there's a university called Universidad Tecnológica del Centro de Veracruz. Es una escuela del gobierno. Y veo en la internet que abren la carrera de ingeniería en mecánica automotriz. Y yo me intereso por la carrera, pido información, traígo mi ficha, hago el examen de admisión, y entro a la universidad. Ahorita estoy en el sexto semestre *and is going very well.*

> It is a public university. And I noticed on the Internet that they launched the major auto-mobile mechanical engineering. I became interested to study that, asked for information, brought my picture ID, took the admission test, and started attending college. Right now, I am in my sixth semester.

> I'm glad I decided to move 'cause I could have stayed and continue doing what I was doing, but I decided to move to start again. I think I took the opportunity and I did it well. My mom is happy with what I'm doing. I'm glad I have a job; I'm going to school. Everything changed for me, everything changed for good. So, my plan now is to finish university, change college, I don't know if I have the opportunity to change to a better job.

> I might take it or I might try to go back to the states, I don't know, work there. But I don't wanna go back as an illegal person. I might go back as an engineer. And I might do things that I didn't do when I was there. That's how I changed my mental-ity, changed the way I was thinking. The way I was doing things ...'cause I think when you are a teenager you think that being bad is fun, you think is okay. But you start growing up and you start seeing things different ... things are not the way you think they were. And I'm glad I went through all this stuff, because if I didn't go through all the things I went through, I wouldn't be thinking the way I'm right now.

Julio's counternarrative deals with multiple issues of oppression and discrimina-tion (Ríos Vega, 2020). After breaking the law in North Carolina, he was asked to file self-deportation back to México when he was seventeen (Gonzáles, 2016;

Hurtado & Sinha, 2016). Being back to his homeland and discovering his father's new family, led Julio realized that he needed to make some changes in his life. As a result, he finished high school and pursued a career in automobile mechanical engineering. Last time I talked to Julio, he shared pictures of his college graduation and pictures of his baby girl.

Summary

Reflecting on how these students have learned to become resilient after many life obstacles have become an eye-opening experience for me as their former teacher. It is inspiring to see how these students after realizing about their legal status in this country, they learned to live with fear to be deported back to their countries, but it has not stopped their hard work ethics and hopes that things will change for the better in the future. After all of these years, these individuals have developed their own cultural capitals to survive in the U.S. Now their goals and dreams are focused on supporting their younger siblings and parents. They do not mind if they had to sacrifice their college dreams in order to make others feel happy.

In this chapter, I analyzed the experiences of five of my former students who decided to pursue higher education at a local community college. Mauricio and Santiago had no choice but to drop out due to a lack of supportive system that could allow them to transfer from high school to college in a less overwhelming manner. Unfortunately, their college experiences made them feel invisible and marginalized by professors and administrators. Mauricio could not deal with rigorous reading and writing assignments and a lack of support from professors and staff. Contrary to Mauricio and Santiago, Esperanza, Elisa, and Sofia learned to navigate and to persist in achieving a higher education. These three female students shared how difficult it was for them to survive college due to regular high school courses and poor mentorship from counselors, teachers, and administrators. As a result, they ended up building their own supportive networks in college. However, things were not that easy. For instance, Esperanza changed majors more than once due to her poor performance. Once Sofia completed her Bachelor of Arts, she decided to move to a large state university where she encountered more challenges, but like Esperanza, she also found her way to connect with individuals who supported her dreams of becoming a fashion designer. Elisa was getting her bachelor's in business administration online since her full-time job at a fast-food restaurant and her mother responsibilities made it hard to be a full-time student.

In this chapter, I also discussed about those students who did not qualify for DACA, like Dulce and Francisco who wanted to pursue college but could not accomplish their dreams due to their immigration status and a lack of financial support from the government and their parents. Finally, this chapter talked about how the participants' broken dreams about pursuing higher education led them to develop their own resilience to pay back to their parents for their sacrifices while others decided to start their own families with a sense of HOPE that things will be better in the future.

References

Conchas, G. Q., & Vigil, J. D. (2012). *Streetsmart schoolsmart: Urban poverty and the education of adolescent boys*. New York, NY: Teachers College Press.

Gonzales, R. G. (2016). *Lives in limbo: Undocumented and coming of age in America*. Oakland: University of California Press.

Hurtado, A., Haney, C. W., & Hurtado, J. G. (2012). "Where the boys are": Macro and micro considerations for the study of young Latino men's educational achievement. In P. Noguera, A., Hurtado, & E. Fergus (Eds.), *Invisible no more: Understanding the disenfranchisement of Latino men and boys* (pp. 101–121). New York: Routledge.

Hurtado, A., & Sinha, M. (2016). *Beyond machismo: Intersectional Latino masculinities*. Austin: University of Texas Press.

Irizarry, J. G. (2011). *The latinization of U.S. schools: Successful teaching and learning in shifting cultural context*. Boulder, CO: Paradigm Publishers.

Noguera, P., Hurtado, A., & Fergus, E. (Eds.). (2013). *Invisible no more: Understanding the disenfranchisement of Latino men and boys*. New York, NY: Routledge.

Pérez, W. (2012). *Americans by heart: Undocumented Latino students and the promise of higher education*. New York, NY: Teachers College Press.

Ríos Vega., J. (2015). *Counterstorytelling narratives of Latino teenage boys: From Verguenza to Echale Ganas*. New York, NY: Peter Lang Publishing.

Ríos Vega, J. (2020). School to deportation pipeline: Latino youth counter-storytelling narratives. *Journal of Latinos and Education*. https://doi.org/10.1080/15348431.2020.1745642

Valdés, G. (1996). *Con respeto: Bridging the distances between culturally diverse families and schools*. New York, NY: Teachers College Press.

Valenzuela, A. (2010). *Subtractive schooling: US-Mexican youth and the politics of caring*. Albany, NY: Sunny Press.

CHAPTER FIVE

Conclusions, Implications, and Final Words

I cannot be a teacher without exposing who I am. Without revealing, either reluctantly or with simplicity, the way I relate to the world, how I think politically. I cannot escape being evaluated by the students, and the way they evaluate me is of significance for my modus operandi as a teacher. As a consequence, one of my major preoccupations is the approximation between what I say and what I do, between what I seem to be and what I am actually becoming. (Freire, 1998, p. 87–88)

Introduction

I have always felt love for reading and writing in both Spanish and English. As an English language learner and English as a second language (ESL) teacher, I knew that my students' biggest challenges were reading and writing. After reading some stories written by Latinx writers within the U.S., I encouraged my students to write their own stories. My students and I realized that Latinx stories of struggle and resistance in the U.S. were very similar.

I used dialogue journals every semester as a writing strategy in my ESL class. In 2007, I received a grant to develop a literacy project with my students. It was before Christmas break when I gave each of my students a disposable camera. Part of the assignment was to take pictures of the holidays. I encouraged them to take pictures of their family parties and other end-of-the-year traditions. I asked them to take pictures of something personal around the house that represented their homelands. I also asked to take pictures of their parents, relatives, and friends. I told them that after Christmas break, they needed to bring their cameras back to be processed. When I brought the pictures back, I asked them to pick ten, so they could write something about them in their dialogue journals. The results were an eye-opening to me. I learned about a traditional Mexican Christmas celebration in North Carolina, cooking traditional meals, presents, and good times, but I also learned about poverty, family loss, and loneliness. Those writing projects represented not only part of my students' writing skills development in their new language, but a vehicle to share their cultures, traditions, and to empower themselves through their stories of struggle and resistance as first-generation Latinx immigrants in the U.S.

After my students finished their writing projects, we usually held what I called, "A celebration of knowledge" event. I usually held it in the school cafeteria, where students and I brought traditional dishes and drinks from our countries. I asked my students to read at least one of their stories aloud and they did it. Some of my students cried when they read or heard their peers' personal stories. As a teacher, I also used this moment to advocate for my students at the district level. I took pictures and wrote short articles for the district weekly online newsletter. At the end of this event, most of my students decided to hand their writing projects back to me. Many of them asked me not to share it with their parents. Since then, I have carried my students' dialogue journals.

I did not want my former students' stories to be forgotten or thrown away. Instead, I wanted more people to know about their lived journeys and forms of resistance. My students will always be a part of who I am. They taught me to be a better person. I became their family member and they became like mine. That's the reason I wrote this book.

Book Questions

Using critical race theory (CRT), Latino critical theory (LatCrit) in education and queers of color critique (QOC) critique, I addressed the research questions that guided my book. First, I wanted to know, *How does the use of dialogue journaling allow Latinx ESL students to narrate their experiences in high school?* When I first started using dialogue journaling in my ESL class, I thought it would be an excellent writing strategy for my students; however, as we started reading Latinx literature, especially Sandra Cisneros's (2009) *A House on Mango Street*, I realized that my students could also write their own stories. First, I wrote a single prompt like My Name and asked my students to write about the meanings of their names. However, as my students shared some personal stories with me before and/or during their ESL class, I decided to align some of their challenges as teenagers and immigrants to their writing assignments. Using a culturally relevant pedagogy allowed my students to feel engaged and to take the lead in their own learning process (Gay, 2010; Villegas & Lucas, 2002). Giroux (2012) claims that cultural pedagogy "has become a new and powerful pedagogical force, reconfiguring the very nature of politics, cultural production, engagement, and resistance" (p. 28). My students wrote their immigration journeys, their first encounters with their parents after many years, some others talked about problems at school and the community, and others wrote about their teachers and family members. Using dialogue journaling in the ESL classroom allowed me to better understand my students and their inner worlds (Darhower, 2004; Kim, 2011; Peyton & Reed, 1990). I learned that each individual student had a background story to share. Those stories helped me to become more cautious about my assumptions and expectations toward them and their families. Villegas and Lucas (2002) argue that to establish strong relationships with students, teachers need to know their students. These types of relationships will allow students to feel more connected to their school. My students' stories also inspired me to support their education and to see them with a more humane lens. Their stories also helped me advocate for them and their families since many of my colleagues were not aware of my students' cultural backgrounds and personal challenges (Gomez, Rodriguez, & Agosto, 2008; Redding, 2019). I realized that most of my colleagues and school administrators assumed that most of my students were undocumented and from México. Sometimes I used my students' stories (without mentioning their names) at professional development sessions and ESL district meetings to educate others about the challenges most ESL students, especially adolescents were dealing with and how to support them. Using dialogue journals as part of a culturally relevant pedagogy in the ESL classroom helped my students and myself to feel connected. Villegas and Lucas (2002) argue that when teachers take the time to know about their students, especially from oppressed communities, it gives students a form of connectedness to school that they might otherwise not develop.

In Chapter Three, I discussed the question *How does the intersectionality of race/ethnicity, immigration status, English language, sexual orientation, and other social issues shape Latinx' experiences in high school?* First, I started the chapter with Julio's journal entry about his sister's experience with a racist local. It was very common to hear my students sharing their or their relatives' experiences with racist people in their neighborhoods. I analyzed how being a Latinx immigrant and

English language learner intersected racism, language, and gender discrimination. It is important to highlight that my students and their parents represented a large wave of new Latinx immigrants to North Carolina that started in the early 1990s. For that reason, local community members, usually Whites, were not really pleased about it. Dulce's narrative with her biology teacher represented one example of the many times that my students were asked to speak Spanish or to go back to México. It made me mad when I heard one of my Spanish-speaking students asking his female classmate to speak English. When I asked him why he was saying it to her, his answer was that his teacher usually said it to other Spanish-speaking students in his other classes. I realized that some of my students were accepting this type of discrimination as the norm. Another incident that I mentioned in this chapter is about Luz being punished for not bringing her homework. Like she mentioned in her interview, her teachers always assumed that she did not want to do her homework or than her parents did not care about her education (Gorski, 2018; Sensoy & DiAngelo, 2017; Valencia, 2010). However, what Luz's teachers did not realize was that her parents could not help her with her assignments due to the English language barrier. No one at school took the initiative to find out how to better support Luz's transition to the U.S. Instead, teachers punished her during recess until she completed her homework.

Similarly, Francisco was discriminated for speaking English with a Spanish accent by a White student, who also said that to be in school in the U.S. students needed to speak English. These racist examples made my students feel very unwelcome and unmotivated to remain in school (Michael, Andrade, & Barlett, 2007). I can recall when many of them told me how much they liked to come to my classroom because they felt they existed. They felt like real human beings after feeling invisible and quiet in other classes. Some of them were afraid to speak in English to avoid being bullied or harassed. I also wanted to highlight about the diversity within Latinx students. Esperanza represented one of the many indigenous immigrant students that come to the U.S. (Arriaza, 2004; Menjívar, 2002; Urrieta, 2003); however, most of them become invisible under the labels Hispanic or Latino. It is important to mention that most of these students do not speak Spanish as their native language. Unfortunately, most of these students, like Esperanza, suffer double discrimination, one in their countries of origin for being indigenous and another one once in this country for not being able to communicate in Spanish with their Spanish-speaking peers.

Being a Latinx immigrant and ESL also made my students easy targets of a tracking system that most poor and students of color get trapped in (Giroux, 2012; Gorski, 2018). Due to limited access to the dominant language and a lack of knowledge about the educational system in the U.S., parents did not realize that they could ask school counselors and administrators to place their children in more advanced courses like other (White) parents did. Most Latinx students, especially boys, preferred to stay in regular courses, usually racially segregated, to be with their own peers. They shared that they felt more comfortable around people who looked like them. Those students whose teachers recommended to take more advanced courses usually experienced invisibility and isolation since they were, they only students of color in a predominantly White classroom (Ríos Vega, 2015). This tracking (segregated) system gave my former students limited access to advanced courses that could better prepare them for college (Nieto, 2004). Sadly, most of the participants in this book were not aware about the courses they were placed in due to a lack of knowledge about the U.S. educational system and a supportive system from school counselors and teachers that could advocate for them. Those students who decided to pursue college realized how ill-prepared they were not only academically but also emotionally (Coulter & Smith, 2006).

Latinx students' narratives about their sexual orientation in high school and how it intersects other layers of oppression (racism, classism, heterosexism, nationalism, linguicism, sexism) and resistance has been barely explored in academia (Wimberly, 2015). For instance, both Dulce and Antonio suffered multiple forms of discrimination. Antonio shared about being harassed by his own peers at school for being openly gay. Although he mentioned that he did not pay attention to his peers' comments, it was obvious that thinking about those incidents made him feel uncomfortable. Contrary, Dulce always hid her sexual orientation to avoid being disowned by her parents and relatives. When I asked her about her boyfriend when she was still my student, she shared that she dated him to please her parents basically. She mentioned having sexual attraction toward girls when she was younger back in México, but she never did or said anything to her relatives to avoid being rejected. Both Antonio and Dulce moved away from their parents' homes to live their sexuality in a less threatening environment. Borges (2019) suggests that, "home can certainly be a space that upholds oppressive systems, like heterosexuality, heteropatriarchy, and gender binarism" (p. 72). Even though they both mentioned that their parents knew about their sexuality, both parents decided not to talk about it. The other form of discrimination comes from mainstream society for being Latinx and undocumented. Antonio qualified to receive Deferred Action for Childhood Arrivals (DACA), but he found it was too expensive to pursue college since he was told that he needed to pay out-of-state tuition. Instead, he decided to get a new job in retail in a larger city and become independent from his mom and two brothers. Dulce did not qualify to benefit from DACA due to her age of arrival to the U.S. She mentioned that her mother offered to pay for her college; however, she felt her mom had to pay a lot of money for her college education. She decided to continue working as she did even before graduating from high school. She worked at furniture factories. Last time I heard from her; she was working in construction where she was probably the only female worker.

One of the biggest drives to write this book was to document what had happened to my former students after they completed high school. In my previous book (Ríos Vega, 2015), one of my concluding remarks was that obtaining a high school diploma was not enough. As a result, in Chapter Four, I analyzed my third research question *How does the educational experience of Latinx students in high school prepares them to pursue post-secondary education and access upper social mobility?* I knew some of my students had decided to pursue college; others started working in low-wage jobs, some started their own families, and few of them went back to their homelands to continue their higher education. I biggest concern was to find out how prepared they felt to pursue either higher education or to find a decent job.

Mauricio, Esperanza, Elisa, Santiago, Sofia, and Luz decided to pursue higher education after high school graduation. All of them had big dreams to become professionals to support their parents and to become positive role models in their families. Unfortunately, higher education was not what they expected. Mauricio realized that some of the courses that he took in high school did not prepare him for college. He shared that he never received any type of seminar or lecture at his high school that could prepare him to navigate college life. He found college courses overwhelming, especially the multiple reading and writing assignments he had to turn in. Also, he did not have enough knowledge about the career he thought he was interested in pursuing, mechanical engineering. When he started taking courses, he realized that he did not like to handle electrical wires. This is another example of lack of information about what he thought he wanted to pursue. Finally, Mauricio dropped out of college. During his interview, he showed his frustration about his decision since he had to get a job a mattress factory to pay his student loan back.

Santiago's narrative about dropping out of college was mostly based on feeling invisible by his professors. Also, he missed having the supportive system that he received by some of his teachers at the high school. However, it is evident that he had a lack of knowledge about college life. He never mentioned about having a mentor in college or a place like a student center where he could go if he needed some advice or mentorship. After he dropped out, he started working at an auto parts store. During his interview, he was still working in the same store but thinking about starting a family business with his father. Similarly, Luz started attending a local community college part-time. However, during her second year, she got sick and missed a couple of weeks of instruction. When she wanted to return to college, she realized that she was not allowed to complete her semester due to her many absences. Another challenge was her out-of-state-tuition fees.

Although she qualified to receive DACA, she still needed to pay college fees and support her parents financially. After some much frustration, she decided to drop out of college.

At the beginning Sofia was told that she could not pursue higher education due to the fact that she was undocumented. She continued working as a manager at McDonald's until she started taking online courses through her job. As a full-time employee and single mother, she had no choice but to take one course online, making her a part-time student.

Esperanza's narratives showed how hard it was for her to remain in college. She shared how difficult it was to be a college student due to her low performance in English. College was too rigorous for her. This led her to change majors more than once until she completed 45 credits and then transferred to a four-year private university to complete her career in Criminal Justice with a minor in Law Enforcement. Her goal is to graduate in May 2020.

Gloria and Julio moved back to their homeland to continue their education. Gloria started attending a private/religious university. She found it very difficult at the beginning since she had more writing and reading literacy skills in English than Spanish. It took her a long time to relearn about punctuation marks and written accents in her mother tongue. However, she graduated from college in Communications and Media in 2014. Julio's hard work and resistance allowed him to complete high school and then college in México. After signing voluntary deportation forms for breaking the law, he resisted and realized that he needed to get back on track and to complete his education. He also shared how hard it was for him to relearn about the educational system back home.

Francisco and Diana did not continue higher education due to their immigration status and not being able to qualify for DACA. After being laid off from work for not having legal immigration documents, Francisco joined his relatives to work in construction. Diana's dream to study cosmetology did not become true when she realized that she needed to pay out-of-state tuition. Instead, she decided to move away from her parents' house to date her boyfriend. Diana is now a mother of two, a girl and a boy.

As I mentioned previously, Antonio and Dulce did not pursue college either. Although Antonio qualified to receive DACA, he decided to get a job in retail since he found paying out-of-state tuition to attend college was too expensive. He moved to a larger city in North Carolina. Dulce did not qualify to receive DACA, so she continued working at a fast-food restaurant, factories, and recently in construction.

By the time I finished writing this book, Elisa was the only student who had graduated from college in the U.S. After learning how to navigate and to advocate for herself, she shared how ill-prepared she felt after she completed high school. She shared how much she struggled with the English language and support at college. She did a lot of reading online to find out how to navigate college and how to transfer to a large state university. Elisa has a degree in Fashion Design. After the interview, she and Santiago invited me to their house where their mother prepared a delicious Dominican lunch for all of us. Also, I had to opportunity to see her fashion designs and to talk about her and Santiago's future plans.

Major Implications

High school never really had any meaning until my last years. To me high school was just another school to attend before I went out to the workforce. Not until I started participating in after-school programs that Mr. Ríos led at the time. Even though Mr. Ríos was not my teacher through my schedule, he was a teacher in my life. With every project or activity, we took on, I learned both about how to show leadership and how to be a generally good person. I can sit and write about every memory we have created at every gathering, but they will all tell the same story, Mr. Ríos was teaching all of us about life. No direct words came out often, but I believe this is why most of his students actually took a lot from him. We didn't notice at the time, but he had all of us under his wings. Being Latino with non-English speaking parents that didn't know much about how schoolworked made it kind of tough at some points. That all changed when Mr. Ríos opened his doors to us. I could go and have personal talks and come out brave and ready to take on the world or knocked back down to earth and quit messing up my life. Having him there was critical to my maturing stages. I don't think there's anyone who left his class without taking something. Mr. Ríos was our father figure at school. The man who couldn't lie to or hide anything from. Everyone knew about him and knew him well that now it's even weird calling him Doctor.

José Pérez-September 9, 2017

Love and Connectedness

José was not an ESL student, but he became the president of an after extracurricular club. As a teacher helping minoritized students fill college and university application forms, I realized that most of them, especially Latinx students did not qualify to get awards or scholarships since they did not have background experience in school clubs or volunteerism in the community. I learned that most of them did not feel welcome in those school clubs since most of the members were White students. To support ESL and Latinx students I founded AHS International Club. This club (space) also allowed other Latinx and other minoritized students to find a sense of connectedness. My ESL classroom was the space where minoritized students felt empowered and loved. hooks (2003) posits that, "when as teachers we teach with love, combining care, commitment, knowledge, responsibility, respect, and trust, we are often able to enter the classroom and go straight to the heart of the matter" (p. 134).

In my ESL classroom, my former students and club members could talk about their school and community projects. They became leaders not only at school but also in the community. They volunteered at community events and also brought happiness to children and senior adults through children's festivals, Thanksgiving events, Christmas parade, and Hispanic Heritage Gala Night.

My ESL classroom was also the place where my students felt like a big *familia*. In Chapter Three, Elisa, Gloria, Diana, and Antonio talked about how much they enjoyed being in the ESL classroom since they felt they could be themselves, where they could speak their native language, and talk about their personal problems without being looked down or ignored. They were also able to talk to one another. Sofia shared how much they liked to have someone who could speak their native language and understand their problems. Additionally, Julio mentioned how he could dress and express himself the way he wanted without being punished. He also mentioned being able to speak English without fear of being laughed at. Julio's and Diana's remarks about the ESL as a place where they were accepted showed the reason why teaching with love was always being part of my teaching journey in the U.S. hooks (2003) claims that, "love in the classroom prepares teachers and students to open their minds and hearts" (p. 137).

Knowing my former students' backgrounds about poverty and loneliness before coming to this country. Then learning about how they risked their lives while coming to this country to reunite with their parents, reading about their experiences with discrimination and marginalization in this country, similar to the ones I was experiencing as Latinx teacher, empowered me to develop love and connectedness. I could never imagine how much suffering most of my students had been through before coming to this country until they talked about it in my classroom or wrote about it in their dialogue journals. My students taught me to love my profession and to care about them as my own children. As a big family, we empowered one another to resist oppression and marginalization.

Latinx Education and Schooling

Reflecting on what my former students wrote when they were still in high school made me understand how minoritized students, usually African American and Latinx, are victims of a tracking system called schooling (banking method) (Freire, 1998). Those who refused to conform with school rules and policies become easy targets to perpetuate them culturally deficient or lazy. Latinx students documented or undocumented prefer to quit speaking their mother tongue to avoid being marginalized for not speaking the dominant language. However, there is more beyond the dominant language. The buzz word is now "academic language," which translates White and middle class. The message is clear that in order to speak academic English, you must be White and middle class, or at least internalize White and middle-class English as the norm to succeed academically or to find a decent job in the U.S.

When immigrant Latinx students attend our public-school system, they do not possess the knowledge to understand our schooling (banking) system. Latinx parents are not aware that their children, especially when they do not speak the dominant language, are placed in regular classes. Although Latinx students have dreams of attending college and become professionals, they ignored that those regular courses will not prepare them for college. In Chapter Four, I discussed how some of them realized about this tracking system when they were already seniors, which was kind of late. They resented that counselors did not talk to them about it when they first started attending high school. Those students who decided to pursue college discovered how ill-prepared they were to face college demands. Undocumented Latinx students shared how a lack of information about attending a local community college prevented them from pursuing their academic goals. It is obvious that these students did not build a navigational capital that could allow them to transition from high school to college. Instead, they went by what they heard in the streets about college admission and undocumented students, especially those who did not benefit from DACA. Unfortunately, most undocumented or documented Latinx decide not to pursue college. Documented Latinx students who develop a strong navigational capital through teachers, older siblings, or friends learn about taking advanced courses and getting good grades that can make them college candidates (Reyes III & Her, 2010; Stanton-Salazar, 1997, 2001). Undocumented Latinx who qualify to receive DACA and decide to pursue college, encounter bigger challenges. Besides paying for their own college fees, sometimes out-of-state tuition, they still have to work to support their own education and sometimes to support their parents and younger siblings. They also know that due to their immigration status in the country, they cannot obtain certain state licenses or take some required tests that could entitle them as professionals in their fields and move up the social ladder.

Resistance and Hope

Freire (2009) claimed that, "Hope is rooted in men's incompletion, from which they move out in constant search—a search which can be carried out only in communion with others" (p. 91). When I was still a teacher, I had the opportunity to visit México as a community leader organized by The Center for International Understanding in North Carolina. In that group there participants from different government and non-profit agencies visited México City and Guanajuato. As a Latinx immigrant to the U.S., this trip to México allowed me to reflect on my own privileges as an educated and middle-class man, living and working as an educator and volunteering as a community leader. I met wonderful and courageous people who cared and inspired others to be resistant regardless of life hurdles. But I also visited and met people that did not understand the word Hope. Their only hope was to immigrate to the U.S. looking for a better life. Then I understood why many of my students and their parents leave their homelands behind to find their own Hopes.

As a teacher, I knew that getting an education represented that hope my students' parents wanted them to accomplish. Many parents sent their children to school to learn English so they could help out at home, work, or in their neighborhoods. Some parents did not know that education in this country was more than learning a new language, but science, algebra, history, and technology. My students' hard work in school was to follow their parents' hopes for a better future. Parents worked long hours and/or had more than one job to support their children's education. Some of my students also had part-time jobs to support their parents and younger siblings. Others had to skip school sometimes to help their parents translating at hospitals, courts, or babysit their younger siblings when their parents had to work.

Hope was always there. Hope to graduate from high school and attend college. Hope to become engineers, architects, dancers, teachers, immigration attorneys, and computer technicians to support their parents, siblings, and to become positive role models in their families. Unfortunately, most of those hopes vanished once they completed high school and realized how hard it was for most of them to pursue higher education. Most of my ESL students lacked financial support from the federal government and their parents, not being able to qualify to receive DACA benefits, felt isolated and marginalized by instructors at local community colleges, for not having a strong supportive system to navigate higher education, and some others felt a sense of moral obligation to pay their parents back for what they did for them when they were younger.

Regardless of all of these mentioned life challenges, most of these students resisted and developed new Hopes. Diana and Sofia found hope in their children's well-being and future education. Diana became a full-time mother of two children and Sofia was a full-time manager at a fast-food restaurant, a part-time online college student, and a single mother. By the time I wrote this book, Mauricio graduated from a private barber school and passed the state test that entitled him as a professional barber in North Carolina. Francisco, Antonio, Dulce, and Luz wanted to continue working hard to pay back to their parents. Julio became a father and hoped to come back to the U.S. to visit his mom and younger sister. Esperanza was expecting to graduate in May 2020 with a degree in Criminal Justice with a minor in Law Enforcement. She is still in touch with her biological parents back in Guatemala but can hardly talk to them in Akateco since she has lost most of her indigenous language. Instead, she talks to her sisters in Spanish. Santiago wanted to start a new business with his father. Last time I heard from Gloria, she was dating a Spanish man and had plans to move to Spain with him.

Final Words

What started as an ESL writing project turned into this book. After more than ten years now, I still have clear memories of my former students and their families. Selecting and sorting out their journal entries allowed me to reconnect with them and to reflect on my teaching journey and personal life. Being able to interview them and using their journals as a springboard to reflect on their education helped us to revisit our collective memories of discrimination, isolation, oppression, as well as resistance and hope. Writing this book had also a moral obligation, *una deuda pendiente* (a pending debt). As a teacher, I promised myself that I would echo my students' voices in a large stage. Now, that promise has been accomplished. This road has not been easy since I debated many times whether this book should be published or not. However, after revising my students' stories and interviewing them, I discovered the importance of documenting and publishing Latinx students' counternarratives to fill in the gap in academia. Many studies document the narratives of Latinx students during school K-12 in the U.S. Few teachers and scholars get a chance to reconnect with former students and engage in critical conversations about their educational experiences during and post-high school. I found myself as a privileged teacher who still has an impact on his former students. After many years, my students and are still connected to one another, now by social media.

In my previous book (Ríos Vega, 2015), I concluded that even though all of the participants (Latino males) in my study remained in high school, they were not ready to pursue higher education. This book has probed my previous comments. Mauricio, Santiago, and Luz were eager to further their college education; however, they felt ill-prepared to accomplish their dreams once they started attending a local community college. Esperanza and Elisa experienced a lot of difficulties getting used to college academic demands. They had to learn to navigate college on their own, stayed more than two years at local community colleges until they finally transferred to four-year institutions to complete their careers.

It is my hope that this book will serve teachers, school administrators, counselors, stakeholders, parents, and interested individuals to get to know minoritized students, especially ESL and Latinx students. Instead of seeing them as culturally deficient or using terms such as "language barrier" and "academic language," these students' native languages should be seen as cultural and professional assets in the schools and communities. ESL students' counternarratives should be used as eye openers to better understand our students' cultural backgrounds, challenges at school and home, and how to better prepare them to succeed academically and professionally post-high school. Their narratives can also help us to connect with them as human beings and to empower ourselves to fight for social justice in education. Their stories of resistance and hope are not limited to Latinx communities. Those of us who have been marginalized or oppressed with issues of class, gender, social status, ability, religion, and sexual orientation have learned to develop our own systems of resistance to craft our own Hopes of a better future. It is this connectedness that my former ESL students and I developed that helped up resist and HOPE for a better mañana (tomorrow).

References

Arriaza, G. (2004). Welcome to the front seat: Racial identity and Mesoamerican immigrants. *Journal of Latinos and Education*, 3(4), 251–265.

Borges, S. (2019). "We have to do *a lot* of healing": LGBTQ migrant Latinas resisting and healing from systemic violence. *Journal of Lesbian Studies*, DOI:10.1080/10894160.2019.1622 931

Cisneros, S. (2009). *The house on mango street.* New York, NY: Vintage Books.

Coulter, C., & Smith, M. L. (2006). English language learners in a comprehensive high school. *Bilingual Research Journal*, 30(2), 309–335.

Darhower, M. (2004). Dialogue journals as mediators of l2 learning: A sociocultural account. *Hispania*, 87(2), 324–335.

Freire, P. (1998). *Pedagogy of freedom: Ethics, democracy, and civic courage.* Lanham, MD: Rowman & Littlefield Publishers, Inc.

Freire, P. (2009). *Pedagogy of the oppressed.* New York, NY: Continuum International Publishing Group Ltd.

Gay, G. (2010). *Culturally responsive teaching: Theory, research, and practice* (2nd ed.). New York, NY: Teachers College.

Giroux, H. A. (2012). *Disposable youth: Racialized memories and the culture of cruelty.* New York, NY: Routledge.

Gomez, M. L., Rodriguez, T. L., & Agosto, V. (2008). Who are Latino prospective teachers and what do they bring to US schools? *Race Ethnicity and Education*, 11(3), 267–283.

Gorski, P. C. (2018). *Reaching and teaching students in poverty: Strategies for erasing the opportunity gap* (2nd ed.). New York, NY: Teachers College Press.

hooks, b. (2003). *Teaching community: A pedagogy of hope.* New York, NY: Routledge.

Kim, D. (2011). A young English learner's L2 literacy practice through dialogue journals. *Journal of Reading Education, 36*(3), 27–34.

Menjívar, C. (2002). Living in two worlds? Guatemalan-origin children in the United States and emerging transnationalism. *Journal of Ethnic and Migration Studies, 28*(3), 531–552.

Michael, A., Andrade, N., & Barlett, L. (2007). Figuring "success" in a bilingual high school. *The Urban Review, 39*(2), 167–189.

Nieto, S. (2004). *Affirming diversity: The sociopolitical context of multicultural education.* Boston, MA: Pearson.

Peyton, J. K., & Reed, L. (1990). *Dialogue journal writing with nonnative English speakers: A handbook for teachers.* Alexandria, VA: TESOL Press.

Redding, C. (2019). A teacher like me: A review of the effect of student-teacher racial/ethnic matching on teacher perceptions of students and student academic and behavioral outcomes. *Review of Educational Research, 89*(4), 499–535.

Reyes III, R., & Her, L. (2010). Creating powerful high schools for immigrant and English language learning populations: Using past and present ideas in today's schooling paradigm. *National Society for the Study of Education, 109*(2), 527–547.

Ríos Vega, J. (2015). *Counterstorytelling narratives of Latino teenage boys: From Verguenza to Echale Ganas.* New York, NY: Peter Lang Publishing.

Sensoy, O., & DiAngelo, R. (2017). *Is everyone really equal?: An introduction to key concepts in social justice education* (2nd ed.). New York, NY: Teachers College Press.

Stanton-Salazar, R. D. (1997). A social capital framework for understanding the socialization of racial minority children and youths. *Harvard Educational Review, 67*(1), 1–40.

Stanton-Salazar, R. D. (2001). *Manufacturing hope and despair: The school and kin support networks of U.S.-Mexican youth.* New York, NY: Teachers College Press.

Urrieta, L. (2003). Las identidades también lloran, identities also cry: Exploring the human side of indigenous Latina/o identities. *Educational Studies, 34*(2), 147–212.

Valencia, R. R. (2010). *Dismantling contemporary deficit thinking: Educational thought and practice.* New York, NY: Routledge.

Villegas, A. M., & Lucas, T. (2002). *Educating culturally responsive teachers: A coherent approach.* New York: State University of New York Press.

Wimberly, G. L. (2015). *LGBTIQ issues in education: Advancing a research agenda.* Washington, DC: American Research Association (AERA).

Critical Studies of LATINXS in the Americas

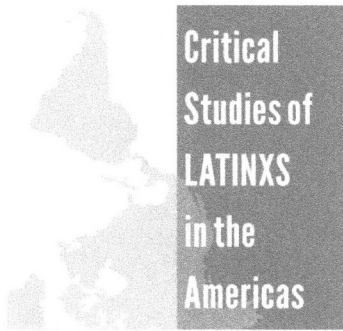

Yolanda Medina and Margarita Machado-Casas
GENERAL EDITORS

Critical Studies of Latinxs in the Americas is a provocative interdisciplinary series that offers a critical space for reflection and questioning what it means to be Latinxs living in the Americas in twenty-first century social, cultural, economic, and political arenas. The series looks forward to extending the dialogue to include the North and South Western hemispheric relations that are prevalent in the field of global studies.

Topics that explore and advance research and scholarship on contemporary topics and issues related with processes of racialization, economic exploitation, health, education, transnationalism, immigration, gendered and sexual identities, and disabilities that are not commonly highlighted in the current Latinx Studies literature as well as the multitude of socio, cultural, economic, and political progress among the Latinxs in the Americas are welcome.

To receive more information about CSLA, please contact:

Yolanda Medina (ymedina@bmcc.cuny.edu) &
Margarita Machado-Casas (Margarita.MachadoCasas@utsa.edu)

To order other books in this series, please contact our Customer Service Department at:

peterlang@presswarehouse.com (within the U.S.)
order@peterlang.com (outside the U.S.)

Or browse online by series at:

WWW.PETERLANG.COM